Circumstances and the Role of God

Circumstances and the Role of God

How God Operates in Your Life

John Boykin

Zondervan Books
Zondervan Publishing House
Grand Rapids, Michigan

CIRCUMSTANCES AND THE ROLE OF GOD
Copyright © 1986 by John Boykin

ZONDERVAN BOOKS
are published by
the Zondervan Publishing House
1415 Lake Drive, S.E.,
Grand Rapids, Michigan 49506

Library of Congress Cataloging in Publication Data

Boykin, John.
  Circumstances and the role of God.

  Bibliography: p.
  1. Christian life—1960–   . 2. God. I. Title.
BV4501.2.B6843   1986   231.7   86-1506
ISBN 0-310-39590-9

Unless otherwise indicated, the Scripture text used is the New American Standard Bible, copyright © 1960, 1962, 1963, 1968, 1971, 1972, 1973, 1975, 1977 by the Lockman Foundation, La Habra, California.

Scripture quotations marked NIV are taken from the *Holy Bible: New International Version* (North American Edition). Copyright © 1973, 1978, 1984, by the International Bible Society. Used by permission of Zondervan Bible Publishers. Italics used in quotations are the author's in each instance, unless otherwise indicated.

Edited by John D. Sloan
Designed by Ann Cherryman

Printed in the United States of America

86 87 88 89 90 91 / 10 9 8 7 6 5 4 3 2 1

To my dad,
who taught me about God,
and my mom,
who taught me about words

CONTENTS

ACKNOWLEDGMENTS

The ideas in this book developed over a period of at least fifteen years. Bits and pieces came from conversations, observations, sermons, lectures, and readings I never would have planned on and cannot begin to remember. My dad, Rev. John D. Boykin, Rudolph Flesch, and Maj. Ian Thomas were particularly influential.

As the random flurry of ideas first began to flock together, Phil and Judy Dodd and Mort and Janet Grosser helped more than they know by their simple agreement, encouragement, and conversation. The main sounding boards were Scott and Betsy Bowersox, Mark and Vicki Cordes, and Jim and Karen Dewhirst.

Rev. Gene Selander, Dr. George Gay, Jay Endres, Marilyn Kendrick, Prof. Michael Bratman, and the leaders of Stanford's InterVarsity Christian Fellowship all provided valuable feedback. Miscellaneous thanks to Helen Quinn, Elisa Bosley, Lori Proctor, and Mark Mancall. Special thanks to Kin Millen for believing in the book, to John Sloan for his sensitive editing, and to my wife, Yolanda, for putting up with me through it all.

WHAT IS GOD'S ROLE?

They have a zeal for God, but not in accordance with knowledge
—Romans 10:2.

Questions about God's existence, nature, and ways are questions of fact. They are like questions about a soldier missing in action during a war. The soldier may be alive or dead, here or there, captured, lost, or hiding. We may not know the facts, but there *are* facts, and they remain, regardless of what we happen to believe them to be.

Similarly, if there is really no God at all, then that is the fact. If there are dozens of gods from which you may select your favorite, as from a menu, then *that* is the fact. If He throws lightning bolts at us for His private amusement, then *that* is a fact. We may be ignorant of the truth, misinterpret the evidence, and argue about what the facts are. But while we are arguing, the objective, independent, absolute facts of God's existence, nature, and ways remain unchanged.

When Moses asked God His name, He replied, "I am that I am," which means that He exists unto Himself, quite independent of what different people happen to believe about Him or even *whether* anybody believes in Him. He is what He is and operates the way He operates. What we happen to perceive or understand or believe about Him is an entirely separate matter.

Likewise, if today we believe one thing about how He operates and tomorrow come to believe differently, God has not changed. The truth has not changed.

When I was sixteen, I prayed as sincerely as I have ever prayed, "Lord, please give me a mild shock in the palm of my right hand each time I'm about to sin so I'll know not to do it." In the years since that prayer I have sinned plenty but have never felt a single shock. Despite my sincerity, mustard-seed faith, and sterling intentions, that prayer was in vain. I now think I know why: God does not normally operate that way in people's lives.

But how *does* He operate? What is and what is not God's role in human affairs? What is His job and what is ours? How should we interpret our circumstances in light of God's activity in our lives? How do we know what comes from Him, what comes from ourselves, and what comes from whatever other forces might be at work? Do the principles on which Christians operate differ from those on which non-Christians operate? And if so, *how* do they differ?

Most important, how do we live our lives to accord with the way God operates?

The questions are hardly novel. But they are perhaps the most important kinds of questions we can ask. Nothing we do or pray as Christians makes sense or matters if it proceeds from an erroneous concept of how God operates in human affairs. Our answers will exert a profound impact on how we think, how we pray, and how we live our lives.

A RISKY PLUNGE

Everybody seems to have answers to such questions. But the answers are usually fragmentary, underdeveloped, and glib. For all our Bible study and meditation, few Christians seem to have explored such questions diligently, thought through the implications of their answers, and arrived at coherent and workable convictions. An easy answer to one question often contradicts the easy answer to another. And any answer that fails to wash in the scratchy minute-to-minute of living has serious problems even if it does make for tidy theology.

This book is an exploration of the mechanics of life, particularly of the Christian life. It came about because I got tired of asking questions without hearing convincing answers.

So I decided to do my own study. I started reading, observing, praying, thinking, talking, and asking even more questions—particularly, "What do you mean by that?" and, "How does that work?"

The more deeply I probed, the more I realized that many of my standard answers and assumptions—and a major part of my evangelical jargon—made no sense. The conventional wisdom to which I had always subscribed wasn't holding up under a closer look; it wasn't sound scripturally, logically, or experientially. And most disturbing of all, it was embarrassingly shallow.

This book is the outcome of that study. I offer it, not as the absolute facts about God or as dogma, but as an explanation of what I have come up with. I don't ask you to swallow my answers whole, any more than you should adopt wholesale *any* pre-packaged answers to fundamental questions. Plenty of verses and schools of thought nibble at the toes of the model I offer; some take painful whacks at it. I can't reconcile everything. But then my purpose is not to pronounce the final word on the questions, but to provide a basis for provoking you to think through the questions for yourself.

I had no idea when I began that the book would end up challenging an assumption that has become an article of faith for many believers: that God works in our circumstances. That idea is a centerpiece of many people's faith. It has been expressed by hundreds of Christian writers; one put it this way: "Behind all the circumstances of the Christian's life there is the all-powerful, all-wise Hand of our Heavenly Father at work. That hand shapes and molds the circumstances of our lives, in order that our lives might be fashioned and shaped to know and to fit into His will" (G. Christian Weiss, *The Perfect Will of God*, 93).

It's risky to challenge such a pervasive belief, and there is a thin, thin line between hardball Christianity and heresy. Yet the purpose in challenging that belief is not to be contentious, but to peel away some unquestioned assumptions to get at the

raw meat of some of the most crucial issues we as Christians—
we as humans—face.

THE EXTRAORDINARY AND THE NORMAL

In the course of the book, we'll deal with three interlocking
questions: How do we make sense of the circumstances in
which people operate? How do people operate in their
circumstances? and, How does God operate in people's lives?

The key word is *circumstances*. I'll be using it as a catch-all
word to mean all of the following: our experiences, events in our
lives, the misfortune or good fortune that befalls us, the
situations we find ourselves in—that sort of thing. It applies
across the spectrum of human experience:

> meeting someone who will later play an important role in
>   your life
> getting/keeping/losing a job
> finding a place to live
> getting sued
> a war going on
> the church pews being filled/empty
> getting raped, robbed, or beaten up
> a law taking effect
> winning a prize
> losing/regaining a loved one
> sitting in jail
> the economy being down/up
> an unexpected check arriving in the mail
> a system breaking down
> getting a date or a mate

So by *circumstances* we're talking about—you name it—anything that happens.

As for how God operates, what we'll try to get at in this
book is how He *normally* operates. For example, I do not
normally get up at 5:00 A.M., wear a suit, read other people's
mail, drink coffee, or hitchhike. I *can* do any of those things and

on occasion *have* done each. But I don't normally. In the same way, God *can* speak to people through a mule, impregnate a virgin, enable a disciple to walk on water, send an angel to spring people out of jail, part the Red Sea, and shock my hand—but He does not normally do such things. He can, He has, and He may again, but that is not the way He normally operates.

There is a powerful tendency among Christians to focus on God's extraordinary acts. He established the rules by which His universe operates, and He is perfectly within His prerogatives to make an exception to accomplish some purpose of His own. Indeed, the Bible records many instances of God making extraordinary interventions in human affairs. He does indeed perform miracles, just as the Bible records them historically. But they are exactly that: miracles, exceptions to God's own norm.

For example, God knocked Saul off his horse on the road to Damascus and struck him blind. How many people do you know personally who have experienced something like that? God's angel told Philip to walk out on a desert road, where he met the Ethiopian eunuch. How many times a week does an angel tell you in no uncertain terms what to do?

Some Christians (and non-Christians, for that matter) tell fascinating stories of extraordinary, inexplicable events in their own lives: visits by angels, audible voices, visions, miracles. It is not for me to question the genuineness of those experiences, only to point out that they are not routine. If you have had such an experience and someone were to write your biography, that experience would surely rate at least a chapter—for the very reason that it is extraordinary. The same is true of Bible characters. Some seem to go from one miracle to another, but if you were writing their biography in a few pages, which events in their lives would *you* record? The mundane or the miraculous?

FUNDAMENTAL PRINCIPLES

Just as we will be dealing with how God normally operates, so will we be dealing with how people normally operate. That is, we will not consider things like mental illness or medical problems. Even though these things and others (such as natural phenomena, the behavior of animals, and the function or malfunction of inanimate objects) can certainly be powerful factors in our circumstances, we won't deal much with those either. Our concern will be the roles of people and of God in the course of normal human affairs.

Obviously, we'll need to get at some fundamental principles. Any principles billed as fundamental can be valid only if they apply across the board to all kinds of people from all kinds of cultures in all kinds of circumstances. There may be exceptions, but the principles should apply in the main. They must apply equally to monumental decisions and to trifling ones. Above all, they must hold up to common sense, personal experience, and Scripture.

I am quite sure it is presumptuous to try to tell people how they *ought* to live their lives. I'm not sure whether it's even more presumptuous to try to describe how they already do live them, but that is my aim. This is therefore an amoral book.[1] Words like *fault, blame, should,* and *right* will not be terribly useful for present purposes. We'll discuss why people do what they do but will not judge the merits of their choices. I'll give lots of examples. Many of the examples will be extreme or political in nature, simply because whenever I explain the principles to people, they ask how they apply in some extreme or political context.

Unquestioned assumptions make for shallow Christians. My hope is that, whatever conclusions you wind up with, taking the risk of reassessing some fundamental beliefs will be as powerful a growth experience for you as it has been for me.

NOTES

1. Making sense of circumstances is one thing; dealing with them emotionally is another matter entirely. There are plenty of books addressed specifically to the latter problem; I'll be content just to address the former.

PART I

Making
Sense of
Circumstances

1.   THINGS DON'T HAPPEN

To understand how God operates in people's lives, we start with army ants. We won't get to God just yet. First we'll try to make some sense of circumstances—which is where the ants come in.

When a colony of army ants is on the march, they set up headquarters by forming a nest called a bivouac. It is composed entirely of their bodies. A few ants anchor themselves by their leg hooks to the bottom of a fallen tree two or three feet above the ground. Other ants hook onto the first ones, then more, then more, until they begin to form long, wiggling brown ropes. As more and more ants join in, the ropes merge into an enormous thicket a cubic yard in bulk. It may contain hundreds of thousands of individual ants. Inside are tunnels and chambers and galleries through which ants carry food, tend to the queen and her brood, and fuss with the endless chores of maintaining the bivouac.

The things the ants do individually and cooperatively with their bodies begin to take on a structure and a function, so we can use words like *bivouac, tunnels, chambers,* and *galleries.* But the whole bivouac is nothing but ants! From a distance you would see one big brown thing. But up close you would see thousands upon thousands of interlinked individual ants.

In precisely the same way, the decisions people make and the things people do link up to constitute our circumstances. From a distance we think of "things that happen to us," but as soon as we look up close we see thousands upon thousands of interlinked human decisions and actions. The deeper we probe into our circumstances and the farther back we trace each strand, the more human decisions and actions we uncover.

Each has its consequences, which all overlap, accumulate, tangle up, and seem to solidify. We call the lot "our circumstances" and "the things that happen to us," but in fact they are nothing but ants.

The first principle in making sense of our circumstances, therefore, is this: Things don't happen; rather, people do things.

JUST THE FACTS

The point is not to quibble over the word *happen* but to root out the ideas behind passive, impersonal words and expressions like that. It would take all day to talk about what each individual ant in the wall of just one tunnel is doing, so for the sake of convenience we just say that a bunch of them form a tunnel. In precisely the same way, it's a convenient verbal shorthand to say that things happen. Shorthand is fine for most purposes, but it is an obstacle to making sense of our circumstances, and since facts precede philosophy, we will need to deal with the facts behind the shorthand.

Our language is full of such shorthands:

> How could God allow this to happen to me?
> Events forced her to do it.
> How can that kind of thing happen in America?
> Nothing ever goes right for me.
> His life is falling apart.
> There's a lot going on over there.
> How come she has all the luck?
> I'll just wait until the opportunity presents itself.
> Things just keep getting better/worse.
> Technology is accelerating.
> If it's meant to be, it'll happen.
> Crime rose thirteen percent.

On and on it goes. Countless obscure human decisions and actions are assumed in each such figure of speech. But sometimes the shorthand gets so far removed from humanity

JAMES H. CONNER

that it becomes downright ridiculous. My favorite absurdity comes from a renowned historian who, describing the origins of World War I, wrote that "planning for war assumed its own momentum [until] in 1914, military expediency dominated the decision-making process, and war declared itself."

Now, there is nothing wrong with saying for the sake of convenience that things happen, but we all know perfectly well that crime does not rise and that war does not declare itself. People commit crimes and people declare war. No matter how grand or how trifling the scale, how many people are involved or how few, how close those people are or how far away, the same principle applies: Whatever happens is the direct result of decisions people make and things people do. "Every house is built by someone" (Heb. 3:4).[1]

Conversely, if people *do not* decide or do anything, nothing happens.

Decisions affecting your circumstances are not necessarily all made by you, by anyone available for you to argue with, by anyone recently, or by any one person alone—but they are all made by people. And groups of people are nothing but people, whether they are a congress, a mob, or a refreshments committee.[2] The legal system doesn't do anything: judges, jurors, lawyers, and legislators do. The arts don't flourish: artists create and patrons buy tickets and artworks.

A prime example of the principle that things don't happen is the economy, because, of all the apparently non-human things around, it seems the least human of all. After all, inflation, unemployment, interest rates, and the like seem to just go up and down on their own. But prices don't rise: people raise prices. People make the decisions in the boardrooms and the executive suites of the institutions that set policies affecting billions of dollars and millions of lives. People make the decisions to hire or to refrain from hiring new people.

All of the decision makers certainly have reasons for what they do, but having a reason for one's decisions and actions does not alter the fact that one has indeed made them! Subtract human beings from the stock market, the government, and any "system" you care to name, and you will have nothing left but their artifacts.

It is a benign form of superstition to imagine that forces and pressures make things happen, whether in the economy, in the National Football League, or in your marriage. Likewise, diplomatic and military efforts will never "bring peace" to a region unless and until people decide to stop shooting at one another. Picketing city hall will never get an ordinance repealed unless and until the city council members decide to repeal it. Nothing anyone does or hopes here will make anything happen there unless the right people between here and there make the necessary decisions.[3]

In maintaining that things don't happen but that people do things, my purpose, again, is not to complain about a word, but to initiate a habit of thinking and therefore an outlook on life: people are not passive, but active. We know that, but we say we'll wait and see what happens rather than make a needed decision—then we wonder why *nothing* happens. We let circumstances determine our course of action rather than roll up our sleeves and help determine the course of circumstances. We sit home worrying about what might happen rather than go out and do what we must to *make* things happen.[4] Worst of all, we agonize over questions like "Why did God allow this to happen to me?" when the real question is "Why did this person do this to me?"

People write the checks that miraculously show up just in the nick of time.[5] People make the laws of the land, the deadlines, and the corporate policies. People design and turn on the machines that function on their behalf. People decide on the divorces that break up families. Those things don't just happen.

One night in December 1982 a husband and wife from Westland, Michigan, were driving home when a fourteen-pound bowling ball crashed through their windshield, killing the husband. That's a pretty bizarre event, but did something bad happen to him? No. A nineteen-year-old man in a car up ahead *did* something bad when he casually tossed that bowling ball out his window and let it bounce down the road.[6] A Christian woman I knew in college was raped in a park. Did something bad happen to her? No. A particular man *did* something bad to her. In 1978 I lost a teaching job the day after California's Proposition 13 passed. Again, it wasn't that something bad happened to me; lots of people voted to pass the proposition (which limited property taxes), and the administrators at my college therefore decided to cut faculty—including me—to save money.

All of these kinds of things are certainly sad, even outrageous. But there's nothing mysterious, divine, fateful, or unlucky about them. People made decisions and did things— bad decisions and bad things, maybe, but people did them.

STICKS AND LEAVES

Lest the principle seem too dogmatic, there are indeed certain kinds of exceptions. Our ant bivouacs do have some sticks and leaves in them, including such things as natural phenomena (snowstorms or earthquakes, for instance), the behavior of animals, bodily functions, the onset of some (not all) mental and medical disorders, the function and malfunction of inanimate objects. There may be a few other kinds of exceptions.

While these may not be of human behavioral origin, they are often the only strand in the web of factors producing a given situation that is *not* of behavioral origin. Such situations are like a football game that is won or lost when a gust of wind deflects the ball on a last-minute field-goal attempt. The wind may just happen. But the only reason it matters is that dozens of normal plays in the preceding fifty-nine minutes resulted in a close score going into the final minute.

Likewise, the fact that we are in close enough proximity to be affected or hurt by these non-behavioral things usually *is* the result of things people decide and do. For instance, while no one knew that a tsunami wave would hit Honolulu Tuesday or that a rattlesnake was under the rock, it *was* a web of human decisions that resulted in you being on the beach in Honolulu or by the rock at the critical moment. And just as important, once the wave hits or the snake bites, human decisions again take over: How are we going to react? What are we going to do about it? How will we carry on from here?

I don't mean to downplay the powerful impact such events can have in our lives, only to put them in context. Obviously, an unexpected snowstorm will thoroughly foul up your plans, and a computer crash can bring your whole office to a standstill. If you come down with multiple sclerosis, it is going to have a profound effect on the decisions you and those around you make for the rest of your life. You may at that point be making decisions about things you would not otherwise have even considered—but you are still making decisions! What kind of treatment should you get? Should you send your employees home or keep them busy until the computer is repaired? Should you risk going out in the snow or stay inside? For Christians, prayer may be an enormous help in *arriving* at our decisions (a subject we'll take up in a later chapter), but the decisions remain ours to make.

Of course, even non-behavioral things don't really just happen either. They too have causes, even if not necessarily behavioral causes, and even if we don't know what the causes are. When a hundred American Legion conventioneers suddenly came down with a mysterious disease similar to pneumonia at a Philadelphia hotel in 1976, no one knew what caused it. It seemed to just happen. Only later did investigators discover a previously unknown bacterium in the hotel's plumbing system. Whether causes have to do with human behavior or not, things we do are often a contributing factor. The Legionnaires who got sick had apparently compromised their immune systems by drinking and smoking.

Nor does the malfunction of inanimate objects necessarily just happen. Roger McCarthy is president of Failure Analysis

Associates of Palo Alto, California, the company that gets called in to investigate plane crashes, bridge collapses, and the like, to pinpoint their causes. He says, "Most accidents are caused by human error. Mechanical defects are very rare. There's a lot of talk about recalls and product defects, but it's mostly just somebody doing something wrong." He gives an example of an oil drilling derrick in Bakersfield, California, that collapsed, dropping a worker sixty feet to his death. Failure Analysis investigators found a tell-tale bent flange and a gouge in the metal. That told them the derrick collapsed because someone had improperly installed a structural piece called a dog.[7]

AUTOPILOT

We don't always make decisions, of course. That's why I differentiate between decisions we make and things we do. We do some things with so little thought that the word *decision* probably doesn't apply. We may be functioning in a mode we might call autopilot. I didn't really *decide* to type the period at the end of that last sentence; I just did it. I scratch my nose or glance to the left or slam on the brakes without necessarily having given the action any real thought.

The decisions we do make are of all kinds: snap decisions and carefully considered ones, brilliant ones and stupid ones. Some we forget in a minute, and others profoundly affect the course of our lives. We make some alone, some in consultation with others, some that no one else will ever know about, and some that affect dozens, perhaps millions of lives. We make decisions in our capacities as Christians, parents, students, workers, officials, committee members, citizens. Some decisions are virtually shoved down our throats; some we make gladly. But whatever their context, merits, or consequences, they are all of a piece: just decisions people make.

Whether we make a decision to do something or just do it in a kind of autopilot mode, the act becomes a component in our own and other people's circumstances. The things that happen to us don't just happen. With certain kinds of exceptions, our circumstances are virtually always the direct result of decisions people make and things people do. Except for when sticks and leaves fall into our bivouacs, our circumstances are nothing but ants.

NOTES

1. The complete verse is, "Every house is built by someone, but the builder of all things is God." We shouldn't read that too literally, though, for Psalm 127:1 says, "Unless the LORD builds the house, they labor in vain who build it." Their labor may be in vain, but others besides God do build.

2. Psychologist Erich Fromm says, "Any group consists of individuals and nothing but individuals, and psychological mechanisms which we find operating in a group can therefore only be mechanisms that operate in individuals. . . . If our analysis of socio-psychological phenomena is not based on the detailed study of individual behavior, it lacks empirical character and, therefore, validity" (*Escape From Freedom*, 137).

3. Economist Victor Fuchs says, "Anyone who believes that the increases in suicides among youth, births to unwed mothers, juvenile crime, and one-parent homes are primarily the result of macroeconomic conditions is ignoring readily available evidence" (*How We Live*, 110).

4. This is one reason why in the Sermon on the Mount Jesus forbids us to worry about food, drink, clothing, and so on. He did say that God would provide such necessities, but He was not talking about manna happening down from heaven. His point was that worry is unacceptable because it is passive. Had He meant for us to passively "wait on the Lord" to provide, then why did Paul, of all people, have to earn a living as a tentmaker? And why did Paul insist that we work with our own hands and that whoever did not work should not eat (1 Thess. 4:11; 2 Thess. 3:6–11)?

5. We are always moved by stories of great people of faith praying about some need and then waiting on the Lord to provide. A check always arrives that very afternoon. They are great stories, and they get us all faithful to see what will show up in *our* mailbox tomorrow. But somebody somewhere had to decide to write and mail that miraculous check. People certainly do send unexpected checks, but I find nothing in the Bible to suggest that God means for us to consider that the norm or to otherwise passively wait for things to happen.

6. "The Bowling Ball Murder," *Newsweek*, July 11, 1983, 27.

7. "The How and Why of Disaster," by Mickey Friedman, *San Francisco Examiner*, April 17, 1983, Scene/Arts 1. "Firm Finds Reward in Grim Specialty," *New York Times*, May 28, 1983, 37.

2.   MAKING SENSE OF CIRCUMSTANCES

Any attempt to make sense of one's circumstances is doomed to failure unless we steer clear of three dead-end detours:

> trying to assign blame for them
> imagining that people should have known before what we know now
> presupposing that life is or ought to be fair

While there may be endeavors when those things are in order, they can only skew our thinking here. Conversely, perhaps the single most useful way to make sense of our circumstances is to think of every decision, action, event, and situation as a point on a continuum. To isolate it from that continuum is to misunderstand it. Like words in a sentence or sentences in a paragraph, each may make a certain sense in itself, but its full meaning becomes apparent only when seen in context.

As a point on a continuum, each situation is one link in a long chain of decisions and actions: those preceding, those during, and those after the fact. Every decision and act has consequences, and every situation is a consequence of things people decided and did earlier.

The roots of the Arab-Israeli conflict, for example, go back thousands of years to one simple decision. God had promised Abraham a son, but as Abraham and his wife grew older, their hope of ever having a child grew dimmer. So he and his wife decided to invoke the local custom of having him sire a child through her handmaiden, Hagar.[1] Abraham and his wife did later have a son of their own, but the two boys never got along, and their posterity—the Jews descended from Isaac and the Arabs from Ishmael—have been at each other's throats ever since.

In 1983 a Soviet military pilot shot down a Korean civilian airliner after it strayed over Soviet territory on a flight from Anchorage to Seoul. All 269 people on board died. The International Civil Aviation Organization suggested that a likely reason for the straying was that instead of typing into the plane's computer navigation system the proper longitude for Anchorage—149 degrees—the pilot may have typed 139 and neglected to correct the error.[2]

An insignificant gesture, noise, or act of mine may have great impact on your impression of me, which in turn will have a great impact on how you treat me and whether you hire me, invite me, recommend me, admit me to school, or promote me. Any little thing you say or do at the scene of an emergency can haunt you for years if someone decides to sue you for it. As mundane an act as putting on your left shoe first can matter greatly if you hear a loud noise, run outside to investigate, and step on a rusty nail with your unshod right foot.

These are examples of bad consequences, but there are just as many good ones. In 1947 a shepherd boy idly tossed a rock into a cave, heard a curious clunk, and went in to see what his rock had hit. It turned out to be one of the ancient earthen jars containing the Dead Sea Scrolls. My wife traces her career in speech and theater back to the time her seventh-grade teacher gave her a simple compliment after she read a poem aloud for the class. It takes only one Supreme Court justice to cast the tie-breaking vote in a case that will affect millions of people for decades.

So every decision has its consequences. It may be a good or a bad decision, with good or bad consequences. The avenues for the next decision, and its consequences, are now open.

MOMENTUM

Today's decisions and their consequences have a pro-found—if usually unnoticed—effect on tomorrow's decisions and their consequences, because they open new possibilities, close off others, confirm us more deeply in both good and bad ways, and provide or rob us of valuable experiences. Once you make the decision to join the army, for instance, you have effectively pre-made most of your important decisions for the duration of your hitch. You may not make a conscious choice whether or not to participate in boot camp, because, for all practical purposes, you made that decision the day you joined. Even if you do not make conscious decisions in particular instances, you are operating on the momentum you set in motion by making that first telling decision.

The same is true of students, employees, spouses, people in all walks of life. A student may not want to take a certain class or test, but goes through with it on the momentum of having decided earlier to work toward a given degree. This class or test is a means to accomplishing the ends decided upon then and still desired. The apostle Paul calls himself a bond-servant—a voluntary servant for life—so when he talks elsewhere about being "compelled" to serve the Lord, his compulsion is within the context of having chosen to be a bond-servant.[3]

One more thought about the decision/consequence linkage that sets up our circumstances. Though you may make a decision gladly, you can't undo its consequences. You can't unscramble an egg. If you decide to experiment with cocaine, you are quite likely to get a ball rolling that you may not later be able to stop. As a cocaine addict, you may literally be unable to decide not to continue, but your very impotence is the result of your own earlier decision to start. In the mid-sixties, the leaders of Romania were concerned about their country's low birth rate. When the rate sank to 56 per thousand (70 was considered optimal), Romanian leaders suddenly outlawed abortion. Regardless of what one thinks of abortion, the consequence was that the birth rate almost doubled to 106 per thousand. Shock waves from that one decision will resound throughout Romanian society long after everyone has forgotten it was ever made.[4]

INTENTIONS AND OMNISCIENCE

It should be apparent that the outcome of something we do may bear no relation to the intentions we had in mind when we did it. My intention is loving when I reach to brush a wisp of hair out of my wife's face, but if my hand surprises her and she flinches, I may wind up poking her in the eye. Whatever our intentions, once we do something, the act becomes a fact—and intentions do not alter facts or the consequences of our actions. My wife's eye will hurt despite my loving intentions. Neville Chamberlain's intention in signing the Munich Pact of 1938 was to contain Hitler's ambitions, even though it wound up having the opposite effect. I didn't intend to neglect the toddler when I turned my attention away long enough for him or her to fall into the pool and drown. People may take your intentions into consideration for purposes of judging you, but the facts of what you do and the consequences that ensue are affected not at all by your intentions.

Lawyers, accountants, and investigative reporters—perhaps because they traffic in hindsight all day long—tend to assume that people either do anticipate or at least should anticipate the consequences of their actions. But correctly anticipating long-range consequences is the exception, not the norm. The less routine the action, the less likely one is to predict its consequences correctly. The best we can usually do is to anticipate the immediate results of some of our decisions and actions.

For example, sometime in 1980 someone brought some fruit into California. Nice, simple, innocent thing to do. But inside the fruit resided larvae of the Mediterranean fruit fly. In time that larvae spawned enough of the rapacious pests that in 1981 state officials decided to embark on a crash program of fumigating vast tracts of the state with pesticide. Helicopters flew in formation over cities and countryside on appointed nights, spraying. Hundreds of state workers changed jobs and relocated for months to spray on the ground. Commuter traffic was halted as inspectors stopped cars crossing county lines.

The Medfly and the program to eradicate it cost billions of dollars, disrupted thousands of lives, and was a thorough pain in the neck for everyone—all because somebody innocently brought in a few pieces of fruit.

And so our circumstances, be they mundane or harrowing, difficult or normal, result from decisions made all along the way. We face the consequences all day long. The idea of long-range consequences for small decisions is, of course, elemental to Scripture: "Be sure your sin will find you out"; "Whatever a man sows, this he will also reap"; "When you present yourselves to someone as slaves for obedience, you are the slaves of the one whom you obey."[5]

NOT A FOUR-LETTER WORD

If the long-range consequences of one person's decisions and actions may be entirely unanticipated, the mixing of consequences of many people's decisions and actions makes for complex coincidences. To many Christians, *coincidence* is a dirty word. It shouldn't be. It's a neutral word. Suppose you were born around 1940 and your parents, Mr. and Mrs. Oswald, decided to name you Lee Harvey after their respective fathers. You grew up quite oblivious to the fact that there might be other people in the country with the same name—until on November 22, 1963, you discovered that another Oswald named Lee Harvey had just assassinated President John Kennedy. The coincidence of having the same name will plague you in all manner of circumstances for years.

Or suppose you and your spouse have broken up. You're crushed. Across town, he or she finally musters up the courage to call you and offer to get back together. Fifteen seconds earlier, though, I dialed your number as one on my list of people to poll for a marketing survey. Your ex gets a busy signal, jumps to some mistaken conclusions, and changes his or her mind. You never get back together. Coincidence.

Coincidence can also be to your advantage. Many times I have seen colleagues needing staff help so badly that they would be quite willing to hire whomever happened to walk through the door next. I've been in that position myself. And we've done it! If for whatever reason you happened to be the next one in the door, you would get offered a job. There's nothing lucky or divine or mysterious about it. It's just a coincidence: two or more incidents intersecting.

What's good for one may, of course, be bad for another. It was good for Jesus (and for us!) that the Magi did not to return to Herod after they visited the child, lest Herod learn where to find Jesus and kill Him. It was not good for the parents of all the other babies in Bethlehem, though, since Herod's response to having been tricked by the Magi was to order the slaughter of all babies in the Bethlehem area.

The point is not that every trifling decision and act produces far-reaching consequences—only that every decision and act, no matter how mundane, has the potential to. Those that don't are indistinguishable from those that do. A single critical decision or act can set us on a course from which we never turn back. The things you decide and do intersect with the things I—and countless other people—decide and do, to result in random coincidences. The consequences of a given decision or action may be value-neutral and bear no relation to the intentions behind it. But the consequences of various decisions and acts by various people at various times coincide to create our circumstances.

NOTES

1. *The New Bible Dictionary*, s.v. "Hagar." Abraham was named Abram at the time.

2. "Errors That Could Have Doomed Korean 747," UPI report in *San Francisco Chronicle*, December 15, 1983, 24.

3. Romans 1:1; 1 Corinthians 9:16. Indeed, Peter says to elders, "Shepherd the flock of God among you, not under compulsion, but voluntarily, according to the will of God; and . . . with eagerness" (1 Peter 5:2).

4. Victor Fuchs, *How We Live*, 19–20. The birth rate did settle back down to the 70–80 range after a few years as women began to use other birth-control methods.

5. Numbers 32:23; Galatians 6:7; Romans 6:16.

3.   WHY ME?

I was once a mid-level manager in government, responsible for hiring my own staff. My assistant had been working for eighteen months in a position officially classed as temporary. Since he was such an excellent worker, I got his job reclassified as permanent, with a nice pay raise. Then I discovered that only the *position* had been upgraded by reclassification, not the person, and that I would now have to fill the position.

No problem: the ideal person was doing the job already. But since this was a government department, the personnel office was required to advertise the opening, take applications for two weeks, administer some irrelevant test, pre-screen the top fifteen scorers, and eventually send me the seven finalists for interviews. They were all fine people, and I took the interviews with each seriously, but my current assistant was among the finalists. After a minimum of deliberation, I hired him for his own job.

You can imagine the thoughts of the other applicants: "Why am I so unlucky?" "God must not have wanted me to work here." "My horoscope said this would be a bad day." It was no such thing! I knew all along who was going to get the job, and I made the decision. There was nothing mysterious about the decision to anyone close to it. But to the unhired applicants—who were distant from it and unaware of the background—it must have seemed like an intervention by God or another stroke of bad luck. The farther one is away from a decision, the more mystical and non-human that decision may appear, and the more likely we are to attribute it to luck or fate or to say it just happened.

THE PUREST FORM OF SUPERSTITION

What is luck? Or chance, fate, destiny, fortune? Are they real somethings out there that grant me favor but not you, or grant you favor today but not tomorrow? Do they cause things to happen? Are they intelligent?

If they are intelligent, then they are gods. And a Christian who believes in luck will have trouble reconciling that belief with a Jehovah who says He is the only God, beside whom there are no others. If they are not intelligent, then what are they? Blind forces of the cosmos? If so, then how can they cause the decisions of intelligent people to order our circumstances?

There is no such thing as luck. The term is a cute but meaningless verbal shorthand describing results, not causes. *Luck* means nothing more than a good experience or result, especially when it is unexpected, undeserved, or unlikely. *Lucky* is a useful word to have in the language, but it's merely a synonym for *well off*. If you have good luck, you have a pattern of good results; bad luck, bad results. Nothing more. Belief in luck (or fate, destiny, fortune) is the purest form of superstition because it has no basis whatsoever either in fact or in theory. At least astrology has rules, patterns, and traditions about the stars and planets and birthdays. Luck lacks even that.

But what about all the inexplicable coincidences that happen all the time? How come my dad always gets the best parking spaces? How come one thing after another has gone wrong for you lately? How come so-and-so just happened to get stuck in traffic and thereby missed the plane that later crashed? Surely that's all luck. It's not just coincidence, is it?

Yes, that's exactly what it is: coincidence. Incident A + incident B = coincidence. Suppose that, as an act of arbitrary vandalism, you string a wire four inches above a sidewalk at night. If I am the next person to walk down that sidewalk, I will trip. Am I unlucky? No. I may be injured, angry, and wronged, but not unlucky. I will no doubt moan, "Why me? Why did this bad thing happen to me?" But if anyone else had come down the sidewalk, it would have been that person who tripped.

So why was it I instead of someone else? Because I am the one who decided—for whatever reason and in all ignorance of the danger—to walk down that sidewalk at that moment.[1] That certainly does not make the accident my fault; it is simply a fact. If I want to know why this bad thing happened to anyone at all, the one to ask is not God or my senator, but you! I may not be able to find you, and your answer may not make me feel any better, but you are the one who *has* the answer.

Incident A (you string a wire) + incident B (I come along) = incident C (I trip on your wire). Coincidence.

To ask, "Why me?" as a cosmic question, though, is to say, in effect, "Don't trouble me with mundane facts like that. I'm special, so tell me why I was cosmically singled out." The question assumes that there is some third-party cosmic force out there that made you string up that wire and arranged for me to come walking that way. It must have carried out its will by somehow manipulating both you and me. You thought you were making your own decision to have a little fun, and I thought I was making my own decision to go for a walk. But if my accident was in fact the doing of some third-party force, then either (1) both you and I consciously obeyed the promptings of that force or (2) neither you nor I really made our own decisions—the force made them for us. And neither of us knew it!

Whether we name that force God, Satan, an intelligent luck, or whatever, we are ascribing to it—not to you—the ultimate responsibility for your action and therefore my "misfortune." You and I would both be incidental to the cosmic process, mere tools in that force's hand. Whether God operates that way is a question we will take up in the next chapter, but for now we can rule out non-intelligent forces. They, by definition, would be incapable of having a will or of making plans or decisions, much less of manipulating the wills, plans, and decisions of intelligent minds.

THE BULLET WITH YOUR NAME ON IT

Nonetheless, we rely emotionally on luck. We tend to invoke luck as the final straw in a tall haystack. Soldiers are great believers in luck, in the bullet with their name on it. But battlefields are dangerous places to be, and *anyone* there is liable to get killed. Any man who joins the Marines, spends months in training, and gets sent to a war zone and assigned to the front is in a prime position to find a bullet "with his name on it." If the enemy has been shooting at his company for a week and then a shell explodes beside him, he will be the one out of the whole company who dies.

The obvious question in such cases is: Why him? But there's a great deal less to that question than meets the eye. It loses its urgency when the less obvious but no less important question is asked: Why *not* him? Of course it is a tragedy that he was killed, but surely no one seriously believes that his niceness or his engagement to a woman back home should make him immune to shrapnel.[2] Decisions people made and things people did account for him being on the battlefield in the first place and for the enemy soldier having fired the shell. The only element of anything approaching luck in the whole episode is how far astray the shell hit from where the enemy soldier aimed it. If the shell killed only him instead of the whole company, it isn't because the enemy wasn't trying!

In 1982 someone laced capsules of the pain reliever Tylenol with cyanide and then put them back on store shelves in Chicago. Seven people died after swallowing poisoned pills. The families of those seven people no doubt agonized trying to find some shred of meaning in why God or fate or luck had picked on their loved ones, of all the people in Chicago. We can concoct some answer and perhaps take some small comfort in it, but sadly, there was no meaning in those deaths. Each was a bizarre, horrible coincidence, nothing more. Therein lies the tragedy.

SINCERELY MISTAKEN

Sincerity does not alter facts. John Connally, then governor of Texas, was riding in the same limousine and wounded in the same barrage of bullets that killed President John Kennedy in Dallas in 1963. Sixteen years later, Connally ran unsuccessfully for president. He said after the election that Kennedy's death and his own survival "played a direct role in my announcing for the presidency. . . . I thought I had no choice. In a sense, it made me feel like I was left here for some reason" (*Los Angeles Times,* November 21, 1983, 23).

Connally was sincere in his belief, and many others have had similar feelings of their own. But if he was in fact left for some reason and the presidency was it, why didn't he win? Why didn't he even get the nomination? Who "left" him? Was some intelligent force guiding the course of the assassin's bullets, steering this one into Kennedy's brain and that one into Connally's shoulder? Did that force want one president to die in order to prepare another? Does God operate that way?

In the end, which is more likely? That the force guiding the bullets and sparing Connally changed its mind sixteen years later, or that Connally was sincerely mistaken all along?

The bottom line is that we are not very good at interpreting circumstances. We never have been and probably never will be. When Paul was shipwrecked on Malta, a snake latched onto his hand while he was putting wood on a fire. "When the natives saw the creature hanging from his hand, they began saying to one another, 'Undoubtedly this man is a murderer, and though he has been saved from the sea, justice has not allowed him to live.' However he shook the creature off into the fire and suffered no harm. But they were expecting that he was about to swell up or suddenly fall down dead. But after they had waited a long time and had seen nothing unusual happen to him, they changed their minds and began to say that he was a god" (Acts 28:4–6). They were wrong both times.

Any belief system for interpreting circumstances that disregards the role human decisions and actions play in producing human circumstances is superstition. In fact, that's almost a definition of the term. Perhaps the most common forms of superstition are beliefs in luck, fate, destiny, and fortune. They show up even in many Christians' beliefs. The greatest danger is to duck a decision, sit on our hands, or work ourselves into a lather of worry about whether a nonexistent shade called luck or destiny will smile on us. It's passive, it's pointless, and to the extent that it constitutes a tacit belief in other gods, it's idolatrous.

NOTES

1. Unless, of course, you knew I was coming and I was your target. The assumption here is that you had no target in mind.

2. J. B. Phillips writes, "Frankly, I do not know who started the idea that if men serve God and live their lives to please him then he will protect them by special intervention from pain, suffering, misfortune, and the persecution of evil men. We need look no further than the recorded life of Jesus Christ himself to see that even the most perfect human life does not secure such divine protection. It seems to me that a great deal of misunderstanding and mental suffering could be avoided if this erroneous idea were exposed and abandoned. . . . The idea that if a man pleases God then God will especially shield him, belongs to the dim twilight of religion and not to Christianity at all" (*God Our Contemporary*, 90).

4

DOES GOD CONTROL?

If you thumb through this chapter and read only a sentence here and there, you may get the impression that it was written by an atheist. It was not. But we are going to tackle here one of the thorniest issues Christians confront, and so we are bound to get into some perilous waters.

The issue shows up in one form or another in the pulpit, the horoscope columns, learned theological and philosophical treatises, primitive superstition, and the bitter questionings of countless people who simply can make no sense of their circumstances. It goes by various names in its various forms: predestination, determinism, foreordination, fate, destiny, necessity, the laws of nature, the sovereign will of God, providence.

By any name, it's a foregone confusion. The terms are not terribly important, but the issue raised is. And whether a believer attributes everything that happens to God's sovereign control or a non-believer attributes them to some anonymous cosmic force, the issue is basically the same. So let's avoid getting bogged down in theological jargon and pose the issue instead as a question: Does God normally determine, cause, and control people's behavior and circumstances?[1]

You can show biblically that He does, but you can also show biblically that He does not. Where one's personal belief falls on the spectrum between the two opposites is a matter of degrees and emphasis. Some people emphasize those Bible passages that seem to say that everything is ultimately God's doing. Others are unable to reconcile that idea with the assumption of Scripture that people are responsible for what they do because their behavior is not God's doing, but their own.

The Bible certainly carries both lines of thought. No Bible writer seems to consider the two contradictory, for they both appear within the same books and sometimes side by side. It therefore seems safe to say that the problem lies not in the Scripture itself, but in our interpretation of it.

Though no Bible writer attempts to reconcile the two apparently contradictory lines of thought, other writers have. The most common attempt at reconciliation is simply to say, in effect, "God does control everything you do, yet you are free to do what you want. It's a mystery." The contradiction between the two statements is not, however, resolved by dangling the word *yet* between them. Lacking a clear resolution, the wisest course seems to be to go with the position that makes the most sense, seems most pervasive scripturally, and squares with people's real-world experience.

Disagreements are not new. At the time of Christ, the Pharisees were, according to Josephus, "material predestinationists, the Essenes absolute predestinationists, and the Sadducees hostile to all forms of predestination, since they traced all events to chance. Material predestination limits the divine decree to this material life . . . to the effect that a man does not hurt his finger in this world unless it has been decreed" (*Dictionary of Religion and Ethics*, "Predestination," 231). Some of the greatest minds of theology and philosophy have wrestled with the issues and have reached no consensus. Nor are we likely to settle the question forever here.

As a result of the dilemma, most Christians settle for a wishy-washy, poorly-thought-out compromise between the two poles, figuring the truth must lie somewhere in the middle. Martin Luther, however, wrote, "I will not accept or tolerate that moderate middle way . . . to allow a certain little to free will, in order to remove the contradictions of Scripture and the aforementioned difficulties. The case is not bettered, nor anything gained by this middle way. . . . Therefore, we must go to extremes, deny free will altogether and ascribe everything to God!" (*Erasmus-Luther: Discourse on Free Will*, 132–33).

I agree with Luther that there is no happy medium between the two positions, and I do believe God would prefer that we be hot or cold rather than lukewarm. But I am going to argue the opposite of Luther. If we are bound to err on the question no matter what we believe, I will err on the side of autonomy. I hope I don't get K.P. in heaven for it.

I'm going to use Luther's position as a benchmark and argue against his extreme, not because many people would agree with it if you asked them, but because it represents the implications of the poor theological reasoning many people do use. As I said, much of what follows will sound like it was written by an atheist. And yet my purpose is not to indict God, but rather the opposite: to challenge a concept that I believe *does* indict God, by tracing out what its implications would be if it were true.

FREEDOM AND RESPONSIBILITY

People often divide the will of God into two or three separate wills. The terminology varies, but basically the idea is that God has His *moral* will, which He hopes everyone will obey (such as tell the truth, feed the poor, and so forth). His *individual* will is what He wants you in particular to do (such as go to this school, buy that house, or marry this person). His *sovereign* will is what absolutely determines everything that everybody ever did and ever will do, no matter what. It is irresistible and absolute.

Dividing God's will up into two or three wills raises a troubling question. The moral and individual wills, sometimes lumped together as God's desired will, are diametrically antithetical to God's sovereign will, both in concept and in content. This is how.

In concept, the desired will assumes that we are active and autonomous: that God in one way or another communicates to us what He wants us to do, and that we then autonomously decide whether or not to obey. The sovereign will, however, assumes that we are passive: God does *not* bother telling us what He wants us to do, but just sovereignly causes us to do it whether we consent or not. I may choose to do or not do God's desired will, but I have no choice about doing His sovereign will.

In content, any given act is automatically within the sovereign will but may be entirely contrary to the desired. Having an extramarital affair, for instance, is clearly against God's desired will. Yet if we do it, then it was by definition within His sovereign will. In fact, whatever anybody does is God's (sovereign) will, simply by virtue of the fact that they did it.

If God does have these contradictory wills, then He is commanding us to do one thing while causing us to do the opposite. He wants us to tell the truth, but supposedly causes us to lie. He wants us to love our neighbors, but causes us to grab all we can get for ourselves at our neighbors' expense. How is it conceivable that He would cause people to do the very things He prohibits? Obedience would then be the most meaningless concept in the Bible. How can we call something God's "will" if it decrees that we do things He clearly does not want us to do? At a deeper level, if God's wills are antithetical to one another, then is He not defeating His own purposes? Do we have a schizophrenic God?

Theologians who argue that God controls everything are always quick to add the disclaimer, "This, of course, does not exclude human responsibility." The argument is that, even though God initiated the person's behavior, that behavior is perfectly consistent with the person's own character. Since the heart of a person is "deceitful above all things, and desperately wicked" (Jer. 17:9), then evil deeds are consistent with that evil heart. And God has every right to hold the person responsible for the behavior even though God Himself initiated it.

Taking a cue from Romans, these theologians argue that people are incapable of choosing to do good, only evil, so whatever one does can accrue to one's blame but never to one's credit. If you weren't already an evil person, you wouldn't be doing all these evil things that our holy God is causing you to do. Martin Luther put it this way:

> Since God moves and works all in all, He necessarily moves and works even in Satan and wicked man. But he works according to what they are and what He finds them to be, i.e., since they are perverted and evil, being carried along by that motion of Divine Omnipotence, they cannot but do what is perverse and evil. . . . When God works in and by evil man, evil deeds result. Yet God cannot do evil Himself, for He is good. He uses evil instruments, which cannot escape the sway and motion of His Omnipotence. The fault which accounts for evil being done when God moves to action lies in these instruments which God does not allow to lie idle. . . . We are subject to God's working by mere passive necessity. . . . He cannot but do evil by our evil instrumentality, although He makes good use of this evil for His own glory and for our salvation.
>
> (*Erasmus-Luther: Discourse on Free Will*, 130)

That is a terribly short-sighted concept. The idea that God works according to "what He finds them to be" looks at the immediate situation as though it were God's first involvement with the person—which contradicts the idea that He "works all in all." Where was God in all that person's previous life? Has the sinner been independently developing bad habits in obscurity, forgotten and neglected by a God who now suddenly "finds" the sinner and picks up on his or her own wickedness to carry out His holy/evil plan?

If everything is God's doing, then were not all the sinner's prior sinful acts—which have been ever reinforcing and hardening his or her wickedness—likewise God's doing? The person may have had a starter dose of sinfulness, as do we all, but hasn't his or her daily development into a major-league sinner been under the guidance and control of the God who makes everything happen?

If Luther is right, then God is not merely *allowing* us to do the evil things we do, but actively *causing* us to do them. That implication is revolting, but is also inescapable *if* God in fact determines, causes, and controls people's behavior and circumstances. For God (or even other people) to blame you for doing the evil things God causes you to do would be as absurd as blaming you for something you did in my dream.

IMPLICATIONS

Let's suppose that God does in fact normally determine, cause, and control people's behavior and circumstances. What are the implications?

If it is a fact, then it is the only absolute fact in human affairs. No other teaching or doctrine means anything independently or makes sense independently. God's all-inclusive control covers everything else and settles all arguments. It's not really true that I scratched my nose; God made me scratch it. I did not really marry my wife; God put us together. To believe heart and soul in divine control is to have exactly one belief.

There would be no reason to vote, since God would install His candidate anyway. No reason to donate blood, pay your bills, feed your kids, or loan your neighbor a cup of sugar. It would be meaningless to arrest criminals, care for the sick, preach, read or write books, study Scripture, tithe, or pray. If God wanted those things done, He'd get them done. It wouldn't even matter whether we believed in Jesus or not, because if God wanted us to believe, He would do the believing through us.

If God determines, causes, and controls our circumstances, then He must determine, cause, and control all the decisions and actions that produce those circumstances. Since circumstances overlap, involve any number of people, and consist of both good things and bad things done by believers and nonbelievers alike, God would have to utterly control everything everybody does.

A friend of mine says that God causes each event as precisely the strategic element He needs to accomplish His purposes. So, for instance, in September 1983, He had an inconceivably complex web of specific things He wanted to accomplish in the lives of thousands upon thousands of people all over the world. One strategic event could accomplish all of those purposes simultaneously: having a Soviet pilot shoot down a certain Korean commercial airliner carrying a certain divinely-selected set of 269 passengers and crew members. God arranged for each one to be on that plane. He arranged for the Soviet pilot to shoot. All the decisions everyone involved thought they were making were in fact under God's control. Their deaths and the heartbreak branching outward in the lives of their families and friends were all precisely the purposes God had in mind when He cleverly caused this one critical event to happen.

Does that sound as fishy to you as it does to me? Quite apart from the goodness or badness of the situation, such total control is indistinguishable from zero control. God could be dead and all the same consequences would ensue from that event. One could as easily credit a stone with having caused it to accomplish the stone's inscrutable purposes. The victims would have every right to ask, "Why me?" though they would of course never get an answer. We would be within inches of a very pagan superstition of gods amusing themselves at our expense.

To say that God determined, caused, and controlled the destruction of that airliner is a classic example of circular reasoning: in the absence of evidence, it can be one's conclusion only if it was one's premise in the first place.

If God controls, then either we do not possess a genuine faculty to think our own thoughts, make our own decisions, and take our own actions; or, if we do possess such a faculty, God constantly overrules it. Martin Luther seemed to favor the former: "Free will is an empty phrase, and God works in us both good and evil, and all that comes to pass is of mere necessity" (*Erasmus-Luther: Discourse on Free Will*, 123).[2]

Either prospect is bleak. If we have no faculty to decide and act autonomously, then we are marionettes indeed.[3] If we do have that faculty but God constantly overrides it, then we are like a horse forever carted about in a trailer behind a truck, never to run, its very nature suspended and wasted.

In either case, nothing we do could be described as sinful or righteous, wise or foolish, because nothing we—Christians or non-Christians—do would be more or less than God's doing through us. Whatever brand of evil you care to abhor most would be morally equivalent to whatever brand of virtue you care to honor—because all that too would be God's doing. Christ's ministry and death would be irrelevant. There would be no hope, only the next round of busywork God orders up. No meaning to life, only the flawless mechanical execution of His preordained plan. No behavior—only function, with no possibility of malfunction. Your measure of willingness to "do the will of God" would be irrelevant, because God would be carrying out His will through you whether you consent or not. You in fact would not even have the option of not cooperating: your very non-cooperation would itself be God's doing.

If God controls everything, then He is creating the very misery, the very evil, we Christians are supposed to apply the fruit of His Spirit to alleviate. We are to help the widows whose husbands He has killed. We are to feed the poor whom He has impoverished, visit the prisoners whom He has had arrested, and minister to the sick whom He has stricken. Dig a hole and fill it up. He is then like the nurse convicted in Texas in 1984 for injecting children with a drug that brought them to the edge of death so she could look like a hero by saving their lives.[4]

On another level, of course, why should we lift a finger to help anyone whose affliction is God's doing? Wouldn't that be interfering with His sovereign plan? How dare we call the Samaritan "good" who interfered by helping a man beaten by people under God's control?

HOW CAN GOD ALLOW EVIL?

A short digression about God and evil seems unavoidable. One of the classic philosophical questions poses the dilemma: How can an all-loving, all-powerful God allow evil? That comes very close to being a profound question. But it's the wrong question.

The question assumes that bad things happen independently of the bad things people do. What is God's alternative to "allowing" people to fight wars, for example? Jam all the guns? Suspend the laws of physics so the missiles don't take off? Silence all the politicians and paralyze all the generals? Revoke the capacity of everyone involved to make decisions? God doesn't exert that kind of control.

It is people who are capable of blithely committing unspeakable atrocities: stacking slaves in shipholds like spoons in a drawer, torturing children in front of their parents—take your pick of human horrors. As long as we're talking about things people decide and do, though, there's no philosophical/theological dilemma (except perhaps why people can do such utterly wicked things).

Of course God allows people to do what they do. But that doesn't tell us anything useful. *Allow* is a meaningless word in terms of God's role vis-à-vis evil. It's not wrong, just empty. Nothing at all happens in the universe except by God "allowing" it, whatever that means. *Allow* implies that there is some autonomous agent doing something that God refrains from intervening to prevent.

There is a world of difference between allowing things to happen and causing them to happen. We must not start out saying we believe God determines, causes, and controls things that happen, and then wind up saying that all we really mean is that He "allows" them to happen. Those are not the same beliefs.

The only way we can reconcile those two contradictory ideas is to say that He sometimes controls and sometimes allows. But if God allows people to do things autonomously *even some of the time,* then that means we do have the capacity to make our own autonomous decisions and actions. He must therefore be overruling that capacity all the rest of the time. He can therefore control circumstances only by doing violence to the nature He Himself created in us.

The right question, the profound one, when we view evil and misery in the world, is not how God can *allow* evil, but whether He *causes* evil. We instinctively recoil at the very suggestion. But we often routinely talk about all the rotten things God is "putting in our path" to get our attention, steer our course, or teach us some lesson. The idea that God causes evil is less a formulated and taught belief than an assumption we just absorb. But if God does determine, cause, and control circumstances, then He must necessarily be the direct and immediate cause of all evil simply because evil is intrinsic to human circumstances. This leads us to further implications.

SO WHAT?

If it really is true that God controls everything that happens, even the evil, then we're left with the ultimate philosophical question: So what? It's like being told by a scientist that all our behavior is a mere outworking of evolutionary impulses: so what? The information that God has determined the outcome will not help us make the decisions that produce that outcome. Since we can't know or predict what God has ordained for a given situation, we can't do anything one way or the other with the information that He has ordained *something*. We can believe that as fact or not. But in the end it's useless information because we still have to go through the lonely motions of making each decision.

It's useless also because God holds us accountable for our own decisions and actions anyway. We can blame God or shake a fist at Him, but if our very fist-shaking is actually His doing, then life is indeed all vanity of vanities and a striving after wind. Life would be equally meaningless if God caused everything or if there were no God at all.

The extent to which I genuinely view myself as a helpless, passive implement of forces beyond my control is the extent to which I will lead a sappy, wasted life. Fate will always serve as an excuse for inertia and mediocrity.

If the information is at best useless, at worst it scuttles any incentive to obey, believe, pray, or live the Christian life. In his letter to the Ephesians (the very one that begins with the strongest teaching of predestination), Paul found it necessary to "entreat [them] to walk in a manner worthy of [their] calling" (Eph. 4:1). Why? Because they weren't! If God's calling were a causing, then He would be mechanically producing the Christian walk in us. But Paul must entreat God's elect to stop stealing, lying, being bitter, angry, slanderous, malicious, immoral, greedy, and filthy. The very fact of Paul's writing must mean that even if God did in some sense predestine you to salvation (Eph. 1:4–6), He is not necessarily causing your subsequent behavior! You can stifle the Spirit and behave contrary to God's promptings. But it's your own doing.

SOVEREIGNTY

If I say that God does not normally determine, cause, and control people's behavior and circumstances, does that mean I'm saying God is not sovereign? Of course not. It just means that a particular interpretation of His sovereignty is faulty.

Jesus always used parables, so let's do the same: What does it mean for a human king to be sovereign? It means that he has the right to set the rules, to tell his own subjects what he wants them to do, and to call them into his service as he pleases. He has the right to their loyalty, time, abilities, and wealth. He also has the right to punish anyone who refuses to cooperate— as they sometimes do. And as we'll see in a later chapter, no matter how oppressive and dictatorial any human king may be, he is *never* able to manipulate people except to the extent that they cooperate with him.

God, of course, is not subject to human limitations, so He *can* exercise greater control in a person's life than can a human sovereign. But one of the central points of this book will be that His working policy is to exercise control only to the extent that a given believer allows Him to. He is a gentleman. For a born-again Christian to *voluntarily* allow Christ to live His life in and through him or her is fundamental to Christianity (as we'll discuss in later chapters). But for God to cause anyone and everyone to do things *regardless* of whether they consent or not is rape.

Just as a human king does what he must to preserve his kingdom, so does God. Once, when Jesus was accused of using demonic power to cast out demons, He said, "Any kingdom divided against itself is laid waste; and a house divided against itself falls. And if Satan also is divided against himself, how shall his kingdom stand?" (Luke 11:17–18). Jesus' reasoning is that for Satan to cast out demons is to defeat his own purpose. But the same principle applies to *any* kingdom, including God's. In fact, the Greek word is *every* kingdom.

If we believe that God determines, causes, and controls everything and that all that has happened in the past was His sovereign will (simply because it happened), then we must include all the things that have had the effect of pushing people away from God. By Jesus' reasoning, for God to cause events calculated to push people away from Himself (and He knows that they will) is to defeat *His* own purposes! If that is the case, then God's kingdom is, according to Jesus, divided against itself, laid waste, and guaranteed to fall. That conclusion, though intolerable, is inevitable if it is true that God controls circumstances.

Jesus goes on to say that, while Satan and God each work to scuttle the other's purposes, neither is stupid enough to defeat his own purposes.[5] "How can anyone enter the strong man's house and carry off his property, unless he first binds the strong man? And then he will plunder his house" (Matt. 12:29). In other words, it's done by an enemy from outside, not an inside job.

If God does defeat His own purposes, then what is Satan for? Satan never enters the discussion of predestination or providence during the sermon; it's always God's hand at work in circumstances. Satan gets dragged in only when we start pondering the implications. We say, in effect, "God causes only the good things; blame the bad things on Satan." Okay, but that means we don't really believe that God causes all things— only some things.

To involve Satan, therefore, is to change the concept radically. No longer is it God's hand doing all the business; now Satan is mucking around in our circumstances too.

Involving Satan obviously makes it much easier to account for the rotten things people do, and thereby takes the heat off God. But we then have an entirely different picture. God's sovereignty suddenly seems chopped in half, since He's having to contend with a rival. In fact, if God is controlling all the good and Satan all the bad, then it's arguable that God is controlling much.[6] Satan seems to have by far the bigger share of the pie.

As soon as we acknowledge Satan as an active force, we acknowledge that God is not controlling circumstances but rather *competing* with a rival who wins most of the battles (even if not the war). For God to control everything, given a Satan, must mean that God is not just allowing but actively determining, causing, and controlling everything *Satan* does! I doubt anyone besides Luther is prepared to believe that!

The instinctive response to the suggestion that Satan's involvement reduces God's sovereignty, is that God is indeed still sovereign, but that He voluntarily *allows* Satan to operate.[7] In other words, God's sovereignty does not require that He determine, cause, and control everything that happens. He can voluntarily grant liberty—dare I say autonomy?—to an intelligent creature (Satan or a human) *without compromising His own sovereignty,* because His sovereignty means something other than exercising categorical control. He can voluntarily refrain from exercising His own sovereignty to the nth degree.

And, I would submit, that is precisely what He normally does. He still could control and perhaps on occasion does, but He does not have to and normally does not. Rather, He grants to humans the privilege of making their own decisions and taking their own actions—good and bad, wise and foolish— and to live with the consequences. Perhaps the ultimate exercise of His sovereignty is to grant us that privilege.

GOD'S CHARACTER

Ultimately, the trouble with the idea of God controlling behavior and circumstances is what, if true, it tells us about the nature and character of God. I can love a Lord who stands at the door and knocks, who will come in and sup with anyone who will hear His voice and open the door. But I can only tremble in terror at a God who knocks the door down, barges in, and starts pushing everyone around. If God does in fact determine, cause, and control everything that happens, then there is very good reason to fear Him, but no reason to love or worship Him.

I can even love a God who controls circumstances once in a while, but not one who does so normally. Does that distinction seem strange? An illustration may explain it. When my wife was a child, her family moved to Italy for two years. Rather than leave their dog behind, they had him sedated, put in a crate, and flown over to Italy to be with them. Most anyone would recognize that act as an indication of how much they loved their dog—because it was exceptional. If, however, they *normally* kept their dog drugged and locked in a crate, that would reveal a despicable cruelty. We'd have them arrested.

In much the same way, I can believe that if God intervenes to manipulate people in some extraordinary case to accomplish some purpose of His own, He is still my loving Father. Like the dog, I may not understand it, but I can take the exceptional in the context of His normal loving ways.

If, however, the manipulation *is* His normal way, then I would have to question that He is loving at all. Any given evil manipulation would be just one more instance of His moral ambivalence. Scriptures portraying Him as holy, just, righteous, and loving would be mere academic theology unsupported by His track record.[8]

I have heard a number of people say, in effect, "Yes, God does cause people to do some pretty awful things, and, yes, to our finite perspective they look pretty bad. But we just have to have faith that He is loving and that it all works out for the best." That reasoning defies credulity. As Harold Kushner says, "How seriously would we take a person who said, 'I have faith in Adolf Hitler, or in John Dillinger. I can't explain why they did the things they did, but I can't believe they would have done them without a good reason.' Yet people try to justify the deaths and tragedies God [supposedly] inflicts on innocent victims with almost these same words. . . . If a human artist or employer made children suffer so that something immensely impressive or valuable could come to pass, we would put him in prison. Why then should we excuse God for causing such undeserved pain, no matter how wonderful the ultimate result may be?" (*When Bad Things Happen to Good People*, 19).

If God is supposedly causing people to do all the nasty things they do, what might be His purpose? Perhaps the one most commonly suggested is that it all accrues to His glory somehow. Presumably His glory shines brightest in comparison with the wickedness of people.

That looks pretty good at first glance. But the argument defeats its own purpose because of what it tells us about the character of God. Do we really mean that God will cause your best friend to gossip about you so you'll learn not to put your trust in people but in Him? That makes Him less trustworthy than your friend! At best it's like a professional football team playing against schoolboys to show how good they are. At worst it's like starving guests for a week so they'll appreciate the dinner you fixed for them.

The idea suggests not God's glory by contrast to people's rottenness, but vainglory, perversity, cruelty, and pettiness on God's part. Recognizing that implication, Paul rejects that kind of reasoning and is angry that unbelievers accuse Christians of using it. "If our unrighteousness demonstrates the righteousness of God, what shall we say? The God who inflicts wrath is not unrighteous, is He? . . . May it never be! For otherwise how will God judge the world? But if through my lie the truth of God abounded to his glory, why am I also still being judged as a sinner? And why not say (as we are slanderously reported and as some affirm that we say), 'Let us do evil that good may come'? Their condemnation is just" (Rom. 3:5–8).

ANARCHY

Many people would feel lost without a sense that God was in control of everything that happens. Amid the apparent anarchy in the world, they take great comfort in the idea that our sovereign Lord is actually keeping control of everything according to His perfect plan.

I for one find nothing remotely comforting in that idea. It scares me to death. It is like a squirrel: appealing from a distance, ugly and frightening up close. It is horrifying, because *if it is true,* then this God we always thought was a loving Father is in fact more evil than anybody Nazi Germany produced— because He produced Nazi Germany.

It is one thing to recognize that life is beyond my own total control, or beyond any one human's control. But it is something else entirely to leap to the conclusion that our lives, therefore, *are* under God's control.

Being God, He of course *could* control everything, but the question is whether He in fact *does.* What we have in the world is at least *apparent* anarchy: people looking out only for their own advantage, cutthroat business practices, child molesting, church members fighting each other tooth and nail, routine divorce, witchcraft, promotion of homosexuality, people being cheated out of their life savings, families struggling to care for retarded children, cruel employers and sergeants, terrorism, venereal disease, teenage pregnancy—on and on the list goes. There is certainly a bright side, which is far more pleasant to look on. But the bright side only complements the ugliness; it does not neutralize or eliminate it.

The world is, always has been, and always will be little more than a whisker away from anarchy. I'm not advocating it, just recognizing it. Newspapers are perhaps more honest about the situation than are the preachers who say the world only *seems* out of control, that God is really guiding everything along by His perfect plan. The world is quite literally out of control, not because our God is not sovereign or capable of doing anything about it, but because He has chosen to give humans the freedom to do as they please and to reap the consequences of what they sow. And since the human heart is "deceitful above all things, and desperately wicked" (Jer. 17:9 KJV), the resulting mess is no surprise to God and should be no surprise to us. *What He's after is people who will be the exceptions to all of that.*

Given the state of evil in the world, it makes far more sense to attribute it to random human choices than to accept the idea that God is controlling it all. One's expectations for people should be far lower than one's expectations for God. I can understand people doing moderately mean things to one another, so I can understand people doing unspeakably horrible things to one another. I may not like it, but at least I can make sense of it.

If, however, I suppose that all the rotten things people do are in fact part of God's perfect and sovereign plan, then I would be utterly confused. I would also be terrified, because it's not just that God is allowing it all—He must necessarily be *causing* it all.

If no one is controlling and coordinating people's behavior, then the present situation of apparent anarchy is about what we would expect. If, however, God is controlling, then many of the things the Bible tells us about Him (that He is love, a God of order, unwilling that any should perish, and so on) seem unsupported by the fruits by which we might know Him.

If there were anyone controlling things, the more likely suspect would be Satan, since the fruit is more consistent with his character and goals than with God's. Indeed, Paul calls Satan "the god of this world" (2 Cor. 4:4; see also John 12:31).

In short, the idea that God directly determines, causes, and controls people's behavior and circumstances raises enormous problems and is anything but good news. If true, it is terrifying news, because it would mean that God is quite literally our most fearsome enemy. Whatever is the worst tragedy, the most grisly evil you can imagine, has happened—and at God's initiative.

A SLIPPERY ISSUE

The discussion of this chapter prompts the question: Who are we to be questioning God? It's a valid question, so here's an answer: We're just His born-again children trying to understand how our Father operates. As I said earlier, my purpose is not to indict God, but to challenge a concept that *does* indict God, by tracing out its implications.

The issue troubles me profoundly. I have heard more than one Christian say that if God is not controlling our circumstances, then there must not be a God at all and their faith is destroyed. I take the opposite view. If I ever became convinced that God does in fact normally determine, cause, and control people's actions and circumstances, my faith in God would be shattered. His fruits would reveal Him to be morally ambivalent at best and malevolent at worst. The popular caricatures of God would be more accurate than Christ's portrait. Life would have no hope and certainly no meaning. I would dismiss Christianity as a cruel superstition and be done with it. And I would do so in perfect conscience, knowing that my very renunciation was itself God's doing.

We've been wrestling with one of the slipperiest issues in Christendom. It is one of those issues on which the Bible leaves expansive room for honest disagreement. It's not that the Bible is faulty; only that rightly dividing it on this particular issue is all but impossible. God operates the way He operates—His ways are a matter of fact—even if we can't be entirely certain what the facts are. It will be the very first question I ask the Lord when I meet Him, and I haven't the slightest doubt that He will show me the elegant solution that has been staring us all in the face for thousands of years.

But in the meantime I have to live with a belief. I for one cannot live with the belief that God works in our circumstances, because the implications are intolerable.

NOTES

1. By *normally* I mean routinely, as standard operating procedure in the overwhelming majority of cases; God's practice, variations from which are exceptional. By *people* I mean everybody: Christians, non-Christians, atheists, believers in other religions. By *behavior* I mean all the things people do, intentionally or not; mental and physical acts they perform, decisions leading to outward acts, and things people say. By *circumstances* I mean any situation, constraint, event, anything that happens to people, the web of consequences of things people decide and do.

2. See also page 31, note 15, of the same book.

3. Fromm writes, "The opposite of education is manipulation, which is based on the absence of faith in the growth of potentialities. . . . There is no need of faith in the robot, since there is no life in it either" (*The Art of Loving*, 104–105).

4. "The Death Shift," by Peter Elkind, *Texas Monthly*, August 1983, 106.

5. One event that was clearly under God's control was the Crucifixion. Although ordinary people arranged it and carried it out, Isaiah 53:4, 6, 10 and Acts 2:23 make it clear that it was God's idea and God's activity. One lesson from that intervention is unmistakable: God did what *He* had in mind to do, regardless of what any human thought of it. The Jewish leaders and the Romans were not believers and did not seek God's leading in the situation. Whereas Christians are forever praying for God's leading and asking Him to take charge of a situation, there is no suggestion here that God did what He did in response to anything anybody else wanted.

That does not mean, however, that He acted out of some inscrutable, none-of-your-business arbitrariness. Rather, He had a plan and a clearly defined purpose that He announced beforehand through prophets, had Jesus foretell over and over, carried out flawlessly, and explained (through Jesus and the apostles) afterward.

God's intervention in causing the Crucifixion is a far cry from the notion common nowadays of God making anything and everything happen—no matter how antithetical to His stated purposes—just to accrue somehow to His glory in the abstract. On those occasions when God does intervene, He accomplishes His purpose. He never defeats it.

6. Never mind the problem of defining what's good and what's bad; or what to make of non-moral things and things that are good for some people and bad for others.

7. Satan's operating is of course within bounds God has established (Job 1:12; 1 Cor. 10:13; Rev. 20:2, 7).

8. Sure, you and I may be comfortably insulated from a lot of nastiness in the world. But the good only complements the bad; it does not cancel it out.

5.

BELIEVING
JACOB'S LIE

You don't have to believe in God to believe that your circumstances are being controlled by somebody or something. People who never give God a moment's thought may believe implicitly that fate, luck, the stars, destiny, or something else is controlling what happens to them. The belief of many Christians is virtually identical, except that we specify God as the one doing all the controlling (and may assign Satan some piece of the action).

In the previous chapter we considered the implications *if* God determines, causes, and controls our circumstances. Here I want to go a step farther and argue straightforwardly that He normally does not do so.

The first piece of evidence for that position is the nature of the Bible itself. While it does record God intervening time and again in people's circumstances, the overwhelming majority of instances do not involve ordinary folk. God causes somebody to do something, tells them to do something, arranges things for them—but it's almost invariably an apostle, Jesus Himself, a prophet, a judge, a king. God seems to have focused His miraculous interventions in the lives of a very few key people rather than in the population at large.

Besides, "examples in Scripture must always be handled with care. For many of the events recorded in the Bible are included primarily because they were unique occurrences, or at least highly unusual. What must be determined in each case is whether the example referred to was intended to illustrate *normative* Christian behavior or experience" (Garry Friesen, *Decision Making and the Will of God,* 89, italics his).

In the Book of Acts we read about all sorts of miracles—

but also about normal, mundane decision making. Paul's nephew warned him of a plot; Paul made his own decisions about where and when to travel; people encouraged him to go here or stay away from there; a Roman centurion rescued him from a mob. Even the life of an apostle was not one divine intervention after another. God intervened to make sure Jesus was not killed as a baby, but He did so by *warning* the Magi and Joseph about the danger posed by Herod. They then made their own intelligent decisions on the basis of those warnings. God was not manipulating them or making things happen.[1]

Even if we nominally believe that God is determining, causing, and controlling our circumstances, we still wind up having to make our own decisions. We can look back after the fact and say that God must have been controlling even our own decisions in a given circumstance; but while we are in the thick of it, we find ourselves having to do the best we can with what we have to go on—which usually does not include any hints from God.

ATTRIBUTING EVENTS TO GOD

David was one who did get direct situational advice from God ("Shall I do this?" "Yes.")—on seven recorded instances in his entire life of seventy years. In each case David still had to decide to act on that intelligence. The rest of the time he evidently just made his decisions without miraculous advice from God.

In the Psalms, David repeatedly calls on God to intervene in his circumstances, and indeed, in the story of David people are often quoted saying things like, "The Lord has delivered your enemy into your hands." But the narrative describes normal human events, people making decisions and doing things. The *interpretation* is that God gave him victory and so on, but the narrative hardly ever suggests that there was anything divine or miraculous about the events themselves.

Even when the narrative does attribute events to God, it's usually apparent that it's a figure of speech. For instance, after

CIRCUMSTANCES

a man named Nabal had been mean to some of David's men, David headed off to whip him, but Nabal's wife intervened to stop him. When she later told Nabal about how close David had come to killing him, Nabal's "heart died within him so that he became as a stone. And about ten days later, it happened that the LORD struck Nabal, and he died" (1 Sam. 25:37–38). There is no indication that his heart attack or coma were God's doing. God didn't "strike" him until ten days later.

A literal intervention of God is hardly required for a man to die ten days after suffering a heart attack and falling into a coma. Nothing is lost by reading the striking as a figure of speech rather than a literal intervention.

People in David's time were generally rather casual about attributing things to God. When David went to the city of Keilah, for instance, King Saul thought he finally had David trapped: "God has delivered him into my hand" (1 Sam. 23:7). God, of course, had done nothing of the sort, and David escaped. Saul's son was murdered by two of his own commanders, who snuck into his house and stabbed him while he lay napping. When they went to David to brag about their deed, they said, "Thus the LORD has given [you] vengeance this day on Saul and his descendants." David did not share their interpretation of God's role in their deed and ordered them killed for having murdered "a righteous man in his own house on his bed" (2 Sam. 4).

Another time David's son Absalom challenged his father by having himself proclaimed king and leading a rebellion. One day Absalom rode his mule too close to a short tree and got his head caught in the branches. David's men found Absalom dangling by his neck, still alive. One of them ran him through with three spears. It was reported to David with the words, "The LORD has freed you this day from the hand of all those who rose up against you" (2 Sam. 18). David did not consider it God's doing (especially since he had ordered that Absalom not be harmed) and went into mourning.

On another occasion, David was hiding in a cave when

Saul came in unawares to relieve himself. Rather than kill Saul while he had the chance, David just cut off a snatch of his robe. When David later showed Saul the piece as proof of his restraint, he said, "The LORD had given you today into my hand in the cave" (1 Sam. 24:10). Does that mean that God sent Saul into that cave to relieve himself? Reading it as a figure of speech seems to make more sense. Otherwise, God truly manipulates our every move to the nth degree.

A DIFFERENT AGENDA

David in his psalms was neither the first nor the last to call for miracles here and now. People have always looked to God to intervene in their circumstances, whether with lightning bolts or with more subtle means. Jesus conducted His entire earthly ministry in just such a context and took great pains to distance Himself from the prevailing expectations of divine intervention. The Jewish Zealots during His day didn't particularly care about getting their hearts right with God and certainly had no use for this "love your neighbor" business. They wanted concrete action and they wanted it now. Specifically, they wanted Jesus to do His messianic duty of setting up an earthly kingdom and (more important) kicking out the Romans.

So thick was the Zealot expectation of a messianic kingdom that whenever anyone asked Jesus if He was the Messiah, He answered obliquely and started talking instead about the Son of Man. He categorically avoided the term *Messiah* because it was so heavily freighted with mistaken Zealot expectations of divine intervention in earthly circumstances. He emphasized the Son of Man aspect of His mission because it was a more other-worldly idea. This is why, when Pilate asked Him whether He was the king of the Jews, Jesus evaded the question and quickly said that His kingdom is not of this world.[2]

The Zealots and other Jews had a sound basis for expecting the Messiah to set up an earthly kingdom: the Old Testament certainly sounded like that was what He would do. But Jesus had a different agenda.

Just as the Jews then expected Him to intervene in their circumstances, so do believers today—on a comparable basis—expect Him to intervene in theirs. But just as His kingdom is a spiritual kingdom, not a literal, physical one, so is His activity in our lives a spiritual work in our inner being, not a manipulation of our circumstances. "The heavens are the heavens of the LORD; But the earth He has given to the sons of men" (Ps. 115:16).

BUT DID HE CAUSE IT?

God's hand is not in every circumstance attributed to Him. Invoking His name falsely is as old as Jacob. When Jacob's father, Isaac, was old and almost blind, Isaac decided the time had come to give his eldest son, Esau, the family blessing. But he wanted Esau first to go out and hunt game to make his favorite stew for him. While Esau was out hunting, Jacob dressed up as Esau, brought Isaac some sheep stew, and asked for the family blessing. Suspicious, Isaac asked, "How is it that you have it so quickly, my son?" Jacob lied and said, "Because the LORD your God caused it to happen to me" (Gen. 27:20).

Whereas Jacob—a scoundrel through and through—knew perfectly well he was lying, we today often say the same kinds of things in all sincerity. Christians—and non-Christians too, for that matter—casually attribute all sorts of things to God that God probably has nothing to do with (for example, God told me this, God put me there, God arranged that).

One of the main Scripture verses we cite to support such attributions is Romans 8:28: "We know that God causes all things to work together for good to those who love God, to those who are called according to His purpose." Notice, though, that the verse does not say that God causes all things to happen. What He causes is the working together. He causes all things to work together *in us* toward His purpose (the "good") of shaping us into His Son's image (verse 29). If God causes all things to happen (that is, determines, causes, and controls circumstances), then this verse could not apply (as it says it does) only "to those who love God" and who are "called according to His purpose," because circumstances involve non-believers as well as believers. How many of your circumstances involve believers exclusively?

Preachers routinely tell their congregations, "God brought you here today for a purpose," and we routinely start off group prayers, "Thank you, Lord, for bringing us here together." But what do we mean, God "brought" us here? Didn't we each make decisions to come?

Likewise, we routinely say things like, "God caused (or allowed) this circumstance to teach me XYZ." I fully agree that God wants to teach you XYZ as a result of having experienced the situation. The only question is whether He *caused* it. I say no, He didn't cause the circumstance or bring you to church. But He does pick up on the occasion and use it to spur your growth. Jesus regularly picked up on situations to teach a point but never *caused* them for that purpose.

If God went to all the trouble of causing a certain event to teach you XYZ, did you learn the lesson? Did you learn it well? Was the lesson worth the price? What lesson might He have had for all the other people involved? What about the countless other circumstances you've been in from which you learned nothing? Did God cause those too, or only the ones you *did* learn something from?

One Christian writer tells of a trip he and his wife made to Israel, during which their luggage was lost. "The Lord knew that as long as we had our luggage we would tend to be content with things on the earth. So He arranged for a baggage agent in Amsterdam to set our earthly possessions aside for five days" (*Knowing God's Will and Doing It!* 59). Now think that through. If God arranged for that baggage agent to misplace their luggage, then God must have been controlling the agent's mind and hands utterly. What about everyone else whose luggage gets lost by airlines? What is God teaching them? Do they usually get the message? What if irreplaceable medicine had been in that lost luggage? Would we still consider the loss God's doing?

One night I turned on the television news just in time to hear that two more men (making a total of four) had been convicted of gang-raping a woman on a pool table in a Massachusetts barroom while other patrons cheered them on. During the trial, the woman was hounded out of town for having pressed charges. I then switched channels just in time to hear a TV preacher say, "And you know what God will do? He'll send adversity into your life to get your attention!"

Tell me: Did God send adversity into that woman's life to get her attention? To teach her some spiritual lesson? What sort of lesson might He have had in mind? What are the chances she learned the lesson? Did the ends justify the means? What would that tell you about the character of God?

DO WE REALLY LEARN?

We Christians all too readily assume that people do learn from their experiences, which is presumably God's reason for "sending" them. But the sad fact is that most people do *not* learn much from most experiences. They certainly don't learn Christian things. They don't draw closer to God, recognize their need for salvation, or wind up happier, better, or more loving. Experience is indeed the best teacher, but only when we do indeed learn from it.

Learning from our experiences is usually discussed in the context of suffering. It's easy to slip into glib analogies to show that God knows best and that no good thing comes without hardship (such as, an athlete must suffer to improve, a child must be spanked to learn discipline, and so forth). Such analogies are true as far as they go, but they often miss the point. Most suffering is meaningless. For every one person who grows *spiritually* as a result of suffering, there are no doubt dozens (if not hundreds) who not only learn nothing spiritually, but become embittered, disappointed, or confused if they ponder the deeper meanings at all. We hear testimonies in church from the people who were drawn closer. But we hear little from those who got the stuffing knocked out of their faith by senseless tragedy.

The death of my sister's baby son had a powerful influence on her later decision to accept Christ. I praise God that she did, but her response is hardly typical. More typical is the response of a nineteen-year-old boy named Joey who was dying of cancer at a Rhode Island hospital: "You could say it's God's fault. And when I get to heaven I am going to ask God why he put me through this. If he doesn't have a good answer, I'm going to punch him in the mouth" ("Stephanie LaFarge: Riding Piggyback into Death," by Katherine Hinds, *Brown Alumni Monthly*, October 1983, 22).

People do not question the pain of childbirth that produces a beloved child, but they do question the pain of childbirth that produces a stillborn corpse. Cute analogies about athletes training neither apply nor help.

Getting people shunned, robbed, or fired would be a cruel, clumsy, ineffective way for God to get people's attention. True, some people do sometimes grow spiritually as a result of some experiences. It does not follow, however, that God "sent" those experiences for that or any other purpose, much less that He sends all experiences, including those that don't take.

God need not inject adversity or particular events into your life to spur your growth or to accomplish any other purpose. You will land in plenty of suitably didactic circumstances just in the normal course of living your life—with or without God's intervention. In the world you *will* have tribulation; it is inevitable that stumbling blocks will come.[3] The question is whether you are spiritually sensitive and teachable enough to learn whatever lessons might be derived. God is quite flexible enough to pick up on *whatever* you experience to teach you XYZ—if you are open to learning it. If you're not, He can throw all manner of circumstances your way and you'll never get the message. If all you get out of an experience is a puzzled feeling that God must have wanted to teach you something, then the whole experiment failed. You learned nothing.

WHAT IS GOD'S ROLE?

The notion of God predetermining every detail of everyone's life is remarkably similar to what can seem to be its opposite: deism. Deism says that God wound up the universe at one point and now just sits back and watches. The idea of God planning out all the details of all our circumstances can be defined the same way, the only difference being that all those details would be part of the universe God wound up. God's current active involvement—indeed, His continuing existence—would not be required. As Markus Barth says in his commentary on Ephesians, "A god who has fixed every detail beforehand may retire or die," just as the designer of a cathedral "may die before his work is completed, but it may nevertheless be completed exactly according to his plans" (*Ephesians*, 106, 108). If God determined in eternity past precisely where and when you would sit reading this sentence, He need not be around to monitor progress or personally carry out His decrees.

Suppose I press the muzzle of a pistol against your temple. If I then pull the trigger and kill you, what is God's role in "what happened to you?" Suppose I pull the trigger but the bullet's a dud? What if, instead of pulling the trigger at all, I just shout, "Bang!" and run away laughing? Is God's role different in any of those situations?

Now suppose I'm a hundred feet away from you. Suppose you're wearing one army's uniform and I another. What if there are fifty other people around, any of whom I might have shot instead of you? What if you are the president of the United States or the sole breadwinner for a family of ten? What is God's role in each such instance? I would argue that His role is the same in each: no direct role at all.[4]

Nor does He normally play any direct role in any of your other circumstances, like:

> getting you jobs
> finding you a place to live

getting you admitted to Harvard

bringing you to church (or any other particular place at a particular time)

returning your kidnapped child to you

giving you good teachers/students

starting wars, ending them, or taking sides

ridding your community of crime

sending certain people your way

providing income, customers, parishioners

Listen to Christians talk about how God works in circumstances, and you will quickly notice a persistent and insidious pattern: it's all egocentric. The perspective is magnetically centered on the self and everyone else is but a supporting player chipped in by God to flesh out my circumstances. The assumption implicit in most talk about God's role in our circumstances is that God is manipulating everybody to create my circumstances for me and then, at the moment the pieces come together, I am in the spotlight to make my decision. No one has been free up to this point, because God has been manipulating all of them (us). But now the game suddenly changes and I am free to respond to the situation.

There is a noxious odor of paranoia around that image of other people being manipulated by God to create situations for me to act in. It makes me out to be the center of the universe, around whom God arranges everything.

To say that God does not normally determine, cause, and control our circumstances is not to cast Him as disinterested, impassive, or impotent. It is just to illustrate where He does and does not normally operate. Elijah discovered that God was in the still, small voice—but was *not* in the wind, the earthquake, or the fire.[5] As we'll see in chapters 8 and 9, God is vigorously active in your inner life—whatever your circumstances—teaching, sculpting, and growing you to the extent that you allow Him to. But when people ask, "Why is God putting me through all this?" the answer is that He isn't. He doesn't have to.

GOD DOES NOT SEND YOU PROBLEMS

Many people I talk with are upset by the suggestion that God is not causing their circumstances. But while I'll grant that there is Scripture to suggest that He is, there is just as much Scripture to suggest that He is not.

James opens his letter by talking about trials but curiously never even implies that God is sending them. Quite the contrary. He says, "Let no one say when he is tempted, 'I am being tempted by God'; for God cannot be tempted by evil, and He Himself does not tempt any one. But each one is tempted when he is carried away and enticed by his own lust. . . . Do not be deceived, my beloved brethren" (James 1:13–16). *Temptation* and *trial* are the same words in Greek. James seems to be saying, "Don't imagine that God is sending your trials; He doesn't do that sort of thing."

The idea of a God who would send trials (that is, difficult circumstances) suggests a capricious God; accordingly, James immediately squelches that notion by saying that in Him "there is no variation, or shifting shadow" (verse 17).

"Every good thing bestowed and every perfect gift is from above," says James (verse 17), but he's not talking about good circumstances. Verses 4–5 tell us what he does mean by God sending good and perfect gifts: "Let endurance [in trials] have its perfect result, that you may be perfect and complete, lacking in nothing. But if any of you lacks wisdom, let him ask of God, who gives . . . , and it will be given to him." James' point is that God is not sending the circumstances, but that He does give the good things—the inner things, such as wisdom—that come out of them. God need not send the trials; they'll come anyway. But count it all joy (verse 2) when they do come, because they are an opportunity to grow and mature.[6]

Paul's writings are the ones often cited in support of the idea that God causes circumstances. Yet his letters to the Corinthians and to the Galatians positively bristle with objections to the circumstances those believers had got themselves into:

You foolish Galatians, who has bewitched you . . . ? [Gal. 3:1]

I am perplexed about you. [Gal. 4:20] You were running well; who hindered you from obeying the truth? This persuasion did not come from Him who calls you. . . . The one who is disturbing you shall bear his judgment, whoever he is. [Gal. 5:7–10]

When you meet together, it is not to eat the Lord's Supper, for in your eating each one takes his own supper first; and one is hungry and another is drunk. What! Do you . . . despise the church of God, and shame those who have nothing? What shall I say to you? Shall I praise you? In this I will not praise you. [1 Cor. 11:20–22]

Paul argues flatly against the idea that God is the cause of false doctrine being taught. That would apply to atheist professors destroying the faith of their students, cults luring people into false teachings, Christian teenagers being seduced into drugs and crime by their friends. Paul's words echo long: "This persuasion did not come from Him who calls you."

To Titus Paul writes that rebellious deceivers "must be silenced because they are upsetting whole families, teaching things they should not teach" (Titus 1:10–11). There is no sense here that whatever happens must be God's will or His doing. "Shut 'em up!" Paul says.

The very fact that Paul wrote his letters to combat bad doctrine and practices argues against the notion that whatever happens is God's will or doing. If, therefore, we interpret Paul's writings to mean that God causes all our circumstances, we do so in spite of Paul's own obvious practical rejection of such a notion.

Paul was more concerned with the results. "My circumstances have turned out for the greater progress of the gospel" (Phil. 1:12). The circumstances he was talking about—his imprisonment—had been prophesied, but there was nothing about the events culminating in his arrest to suggest that they were God's doing.[7] He wrote elsewhere, "We also exult in our tribulations." Why? Because they were God's doing? No, Paul suggests no such idea here. Rather, he exulted in them "knowing that tribulation brings about perseverance," which in turn brings about proven character, which in turn brings about hope (Rom. 5:3–4). Paul does not discuss the *cause* of tribulations here, only the *result:* inner growth.

James, however, does discuss the cause. He says, "Where jealousy and selfish ambition exist, there is disorder and every evil thing" (James 3:16). James goes on to say, "What is the source of quarrels and conflicts among you? Is not the source your pleasures that wage war in your members? You lust and do not have; so you commit murder. And you are envious and cannot obtain; so you fight and quarrel" (James 4:1–2). Paul says that "foolish and ignorant speculations ... produce quarrels" (2 Tim. 2:23). Peter talks about "the corruption that is in the world by lust" (2 Peter 1:4). Solomon says, "A man's own folly ruins his life, yet his heart rages against the LORD," and, "Only by pride cometh contention" (Prov. 19:3 NIV; Prov. 13:10 KJV).

I sometimes suspect that God and Satan could both go out of business tomorrow and we would keep right on producing sin and nasty situations for one another on sheer momentum!

HE DOESN'T BAIL US OUT, EITHER

God does not normally send circumstances, nor does He normally bail us out of them. True, "the Lord knows how to rescue the godly from temptation [trials]" (2 Peter 2:9). He knows how, He can, He has, and He sometimes does rescue. But not normally. Peter's whole first letter is about bracing yourself to endure trials, not about expecting God to pull you out of them. "For this finds favor, if for the sake of conscience toward God a man bears up under sorrows when suffering unjustly. For what credit is there if, when you sin and are harshly treated, you endure it with patience? But if when you do what is right and suffer for it you patiently endure it, this finds favor with God" (1 Peter 2:19–20).

Peter's own denial of Jesus had been foretold, but Jesus said, "I have prayed for you, that your faith may not fail; and you, when once you have turned again, strengthen your brothers" (Luke 22:32). Jesus didn't pray that Peter's ordeal be prevented, but that his *faith* be preserved and that he grow from the experience to help others grow. Results.

Now, Paul sometimes does make it sound as though we should expect the Lord to bail us out of our circumstances. He writes that Jesus "gave Himself for our sins, that He might deliver us out of this present evil age, according to the will of our God" (Gal. 1:4). He even says to Timothy, "I was delivered out of the lion's mouth. The Lord will deliver me from every evil deed, and will bring me safely to His heavenly kingdom" (2 Tim. 4:17–18). But earlier in the same letter he recounts all the sufferings he had endured (that is, those that God had *not* delivered him from), so it is unlikely that Paul meant that God would rescue him from his problems or prevent people from hurting him. Indeed, this was probably the last letter Paul wrote before being killed.

Jesus never guarantees happiness, material success, security, fulfillment, or a comfortable life. The only thing He guarantees in this world is tribulation.[8] Singer Andraé Crouch wrote a nice little song that goes, "I've got confidence / God is gonna see me through. / No matter what the case may be / I know He's gonna fix it for me."* But it's dangerous to latch onto the notion that God is going to make everything work out for you—because when the guaranteed tribulation persists, you're likely to figure God's not coming through and you'll fall away. The problem is expecting God to fulfill promises He never made.

Jesus told His disciples that God's eye is on each sparrow

---

*"I've Got Confidence," by Andraé Crouch. © 1969 by Lexicon Music, Inc. ASCAP. All rights reserved. International copyright secured. Used by special permission.

CIRCUMSTANCES

that falls and that each hair of the disciples' heads is numbered (Matt. 10:29–31). The sparrow still falls, of course, as do the hairs. Jesus' point was not that they wouldn't fall, but that God loves you and keeps you after this life.

His context was sending the disciples out on a preaching tour and warning them of rejection and persecution. You will be persecuted, He told them—the sparrow will fall—but don't fear those who kill the body (verse 28) because you are God's child. You do face great risk, He was saying, but that is not to be your concern.[9] Right after talking about the sparrow and the hairs, Jesus says to confess Him before men; don't deny Him (verses 32–33). *That* is to be the disciples' concern, not their safety.

If God did manipulate circumstances to teach us things and move us places, then it would make no sense for Him *not* to spare us pointless and meaningless suffering, that from which He knows we will learn nothing but will only become confused, hurt, or embittered. Some would say that such experiences constitute God's chastening of His children. If that is so, then why do non-believers experience identical misfortunes?

To the extent that we look to Jesus to bail us out of harsh circumstances instead of radically transforming us from the inside out as a result of them, we miss the point of Jesus just as much as the Zealots did.[10]

NOTES

1. There was an interesting case in David's life. He was in the town of Keilah. King Saul was looking for him. Worried, David asked the Lord, "Will the men of Keilah surrender me and my men into the hand of Saul?' And the LORD said, 'They will surrender you.' " So David and his men ran away and escaped. The people of Keilah therefore never did turn him over to Saul (1 Samuel 23:7–14).

The incident suggests an answer to the age-old question: If you somehow knew that something would happen in the future and acted to prevent it, would you be able to prevent it or is the event inevitable? The answer apparently is that you *can* prevent it. David did by running away from Keilah. And he had it from God Himself that it would happen. Though God knows the future, He apparently does not implement His foreknowledge by making happen what He foreknows. If David's experience is any indication, even a foreseen future may be contingent on what people do.

2. John 18:33–38. See Oscar Cullmann, *The State in the New Testament,* chapter 2.

3. John 16:33; Luke 17:1.

4. Except possibly trying to persuade me not to shoot.

5. 1 Kings 19:11–13.

6. God gives the growth (see 1 Cor. 3:6).

7. Acts 21–25.

8. John 16:33.

9. The disciples were under God's special protection while Jesus was on the earth (John 17:12).

10. A misleading implication can emerge from what I've been saying, so let me clarify. I do not mean to advocate the common sophomore philosophy notion that suffering is bad and that any God who would inflict suffering must therefore Himself be bad. I don't buy that shallow argument. Our values are not God's values, nor are His ours. We may consider X the highest imaginable value and Y the worst thing that can happen, but God does not share our values.

Many people believe that human life is the highest value imaginable, yet human life regularly takes second place to other values, such as political principles, vengeance, saving money on traffic lights, loyalty to someone or something, escaping with the cash, foreign policy objectives. The simple maintenance of human life doesn't appear to be at the top of God's list of values either.

If I read the Bible correctly, God's highest values are our salvation and subsequent maturity into the image of Christ. If I understand my fellow Christians correctly, many of them believe that circumstances—including suffering when appropriate—are the means God sends to bump the recipients and those around them toward His ends of salvation and maturity.

Now, if those supposed means did in fact accomplish those ends, then we could hardly question God for sending them. After all, if God sent circumstances and suffering that worked, we could have faith that our loving Father knows what He's doing and cares enough to do what He must to accomplish what is for our own good.

But my whole point is that the supposed means we attribute to Him usually *do not* accomplish His ends. Suffering does *not* work most of the time. The overwhelming majority of the population never gets saved. Of those who do, countless never mature much. The spiritual lessons our circumstances are supposed to teach us usually go unlearned. We somehow don't get around to doing the things God supposedly put us in a situation to do. Rather than appreciate the glory of God, people burned by circumstances more often than not become embittered and resentful. One might argue from a predestination standpoint that God does not intend that certain people be saved—but then why would He still send them suffering? Wouldn't that be pretty cruel? Why would He send saved people circumstances from which He knows they won't grow spiritually?

PART II

God's Part, Our Part

6

HOW PEOPLE OPERATE

So far, much of what we've discussed has been negative: Things don't happen; our circumstances are not under the control of either God, Satan, luck, or fate; God does not manipulate people; and so on. That has, I hope, cleared away some cobwebs so we can now move on to the positive side of the issues: If God is not in the business of controlling behavior, then why *do* we behave as we do? What *is* God's role?

We'll take the first question first: how people operate. Let's start with a few truisms:

> People often do what they want to do.
> We can't always do what we want to do.
> We often want one thing more than we want something else.
> We often have to choose between one thing we want and something else we want.

Those are hardly profound insights, but they do provide the basis for one of the most important principles this book has to offer. In fact, a couple of chapters will be devoted to exploring the logical and scriptural basis, implications, and subtleties of the principle.

It is this: The vast majority of decisions people make (the big ones as well as the mundane ones) can be accounted for by either of two criteria—we do precisely what we *want* to do, or we do what is most *important* to us at the moment we make the decision. Conversely, if we decide *not* to do something, it is because, given the options open to us, either it isn't something we want to do, or something else is more important to us.

Now, I can't prove by formal logic or by quoting any single

Scripture that these two criteria—what we want and what's important to us—are together adequate to account for most human decisions. I can only illustrate how the postulate applies in case after case after case. Nor will I be so dogmatic as to insist that there can be no conceivable exceptions.[1] But I do offer it as a Scripture-based observation.[2] You'll have to judge its validity logically and empirically for yourself. But if it does have any merit, it may help answer some otherwise intractable questions.

It can also make us uncomfortable. I smacked head-on into that realization one Sunday morning when an acquaintance at church told me he was moving from across town to within half a mile of my apartment. "Hey, now we can see each other a lot more often!" he said. "Hey, that'll be great!" I said. But a disquieting thought started gnawing at me: *No we won't. If we really wanted to spend time together, five miles wouldn't stop us. And if we don't really care about spending time together—and I'm afraid that's the case—then being within half a mile isn't going to make any difference.* And sure enough, we never did see each other any more often than we ever had.

By contrast, my wife and I were separated by sixty miles for four months while we were dating, but we still always managed somehow to see each other two or three times a month. We wanted to.

Jesus was realistic about such things. He told a parable of a man who had invited guests to dinner. "But they all alike began to make excuses." One had to go look at his new land, another had to tend his new oxen, yet another had just gotten married. Those were all perfectly polite excuses. Polite, but excuses nonetheless, and the man giving the dinner was justifiably insulted. Politeness aside, the fact was that the people simply didn't want to come.[3]

Paul was equally realistic when the governor, Felix, told him, "Go away for the present, and when I find time, I will summon you." Paul knew perfectly well that Felix' problem was not time but inclination. Felix had "become frightened" when Paul started talking about righteousness, self-control, and judgment (Acts 24:25). Felix didn't *want* to hear more.

We use Felix' same excuse all the time. We keep meaning to have someone over for dinner, talk to someone about the Lord, clean out the garage, or study the Bible, but somehow we just never seem to find the time. The reason we don't find the time is that we don't *make* the time. And we don't make the time because, deep down, either we don't particularly want to do those things or they aren't really as important to us as the things we *do* find time for. We may admire prayer as a fine thing to do, but it's not important enough to us to pray, so we somehow never get around to it. We may feel obligated to spend more time with our families, but other things—perhaps our business, keeping the house clean, television, keeping other people happy—in fact take priority.

WANTS AND PRIORITIES

I'll use the term *priorities* as a shorthand for "the things that are most important to us." What's the difference between the two criteria, wants and priorities? Not necessarily anything. The two are often synonymous. I want to write this book; it is also important to me to write it. Some people want to run for president; it is also important to them to run.

Our wants and priorities may often be the same, but more often than not they are in competition. We do plenty of things we distinctly do *not* want to do: confront someone on a touchy issue, march off to war, spend endless hours caring for an invalid family member, leave a special person to go off to school, obey a despotic boss, and so on.

When we do something we don't want to do, it is because we let some other consideration take priority over our desire. When our wants conflict with our priorities in any given choice, we will go with whichever one is more deeply held or strongly felt at that moment: I may want to devour a pound of chocolates but stop at one piece because it is more important to me to look trim. I may want to speak up when someone disparages my Lord, but I keep quiet because it is more important to me to appear congenial and to avoid making a scene. I may hate my job and desperately want to quit, but I stay on because it is more important to me to feed my family, avoid the uncertainties of unemployment, and maintain my lifestyle.

Priorities don't always win out over wants. It may be important to me to start the day with prayer and Bible reading, but at the moment I really want to stay in that nice warm bed, so I do. It may be important to you to go back to school to finish a degree, but you don't really want to disrupt your life, so you don't. Regardless of the merits of our choice or how much we might regret it later, it will almost always reflect our wants and priorities at the moment we make it.

I use the word *wants* instead of the biblical terms *desires, passions, pleasures,* or *lusts* because it includes them while also allowing for things we're only lukewarm about. I'll be using *priorities* to refer to both of the levels at which they operate: the big-league, broad life policies (for example, fulfillment is more important to me than wealth) and the decision-by-decision grind as new choices arise (such as, I would rather do this than that, forego one thing rather than miss out on another). I'll use the word to *value* as a generic shorthand meaning both to *want* and/or to *consider important.*

We needn't be terribly concerned about drawing sharp definitions of or distinctions between wants and priorities. They would be more artificial than helpful. As a very rough rule of thumb, though, we can say that wants *tend* to be absolute or simple: I want to do something, so I do it. I don't face a choice between options; I just cruise along doing as I please. Priorities, on the other hand, tend to be relative and come into play when there is some kind of conflict or choice to be made between options. Though there are plenty of exceptions, wants *tend* to be more selfish, immoral, impulsive, or short-sighted than priorities.

To say that I want something enough to do it is not to say

that I necessarily feel strongly about it. I may merely be willing to go along. If I'm not doing anything much Saturday morning and you ask me to play tennis with you, I may go just to have something to do.

Conversely, to say I don't want to do something need not mean I have an active aversion to doing it. It may simply mean I passively lack a desire to do it. Also, the thing I don't do may not be *un*important to me: there may just be something else *more* important that takes priority.[4]

The more nearly equal two options are in importance to me, the more likely I am to seek some compromise that retains what I value about both. For example, suppose you phone me at home and invite me to go to a jazz concert. I may have a tough time trying to work out some compromise between the fact that I don't like jazz much and my willingness to spend time with you; between my reluctance to hurt your feelings by declining and my reluctance to irritate my wife, who wants me to stay home. But whatever compromise I come up with will represent an attempt to retain pieces of two or more things I value.

Of course, we often don't know what we want. Most people, in fact, tend to coast along with only the vaguest notion of what they want out of life, what they want to accomplish in the next day, week, or year. Two blind men once sat at the side of the road calling out to Jesus as He passed, "Lord, have mercy on us!" Jesus stopped and asked them a very intelligent question: "What do you wish Me to do for you?" They answered, "We want our eyes to be opened" (Matt. 20:30–34). They, like we, may have thought the question disingenuous and the answer obvious, but Jesus had an important point to make. He wanted to pin them down and make them clarify exactly what they wanted. He frequently healed people by saying, "Be it done for you according to your faith"—and if they didn't know what they wanted, no telling what might have happened to them!

What we want may not only be vague, often it may even be

irrational. For example, talking about masochistic tendencies, psychologist Erich Fromm asks rhetorically, "How can one explain that some men are attracted by and tend to incur what we all seem to go to such length to avoid: pain and suffering?" (*Escape From Freedom,* 147). We won't get into the murky waters of the subconscious, but suffice it to say that, not only do we not necessarily understand all our own wants, we might abhor some of them if we did.

BACKGROUND REASONS

Wants and priorities are the immediate bases for what we do. But there may be any number of background reasons *why* we do or don't want to do something, why it is or isn't important to us. I attend this church because I want to, and I want to *because* I like the people here. It's important to the doctor to prescribe a certain medicine *because* he or she believes it will help the patient. A friend may consider it important to avoid you today *because* of fear that some prediction in the astrology column may come true.

Other such background reasons may be interest, a sense of duty, reflex, a belief, a probability estimate, wisdom, taste, altruism, selfishness, shyness, laziness, uncertainty, confusion, suspiciousness, low blood sugar—whatever. If, for example, I stand in a corner at a party rather than try to strike up a conversation with someone, it isn't because I'm shy, really. The direct, immediate, and deciding reason is that I don't *want* to make that move. And the reason I don't want to is that I am shy.

Whatever the background reason, it does not produce our behavior directly. Rather, it influences our wants and priorities. Those are what we act out. In the mechanics of how people operate, our wants and priorities arbitrate between conflicting background motives and serve as the linkage between those background factors and our behavior.[5]

NOTES

1. A psychiatrist would explore people's behavior in a finer degree of resolution, but for most practical purposes, we can get by just fine at the degree being discussed here. I offer the principle solely as a useful way of classifying our motivations.

2. Paul's confession in Romans 7 that "I do the very thing I do not wish to do" and the perspective of this book may, at first glance, seem to be contradictory. They are not, though, because what Paul calls the principle or "law of sin" is part of the milieu of what we are: it "dwells in me." That milieu will be discussed in chapter 9, "God in You."

3. Luke 14:16–24.

4. Likewise, forgetting to do something I had meant to do need not mean it is unimportant to me; it just means that doing it is not among the things most important to me *at the moment*.

5. A common misconception is that people always do what is most comfortable to them or what gives them the most pleasure. It's part of the "economic person" notion that we always do what yields us the greatest good. That's true much of the time, but it fails to account for the many unselfish things we do. Fromm says, "Many psychologists have assumed that the experience of pleasure and the avoidance of pain is the only legitimate principle guiding human action; but dynamic psychology can show that the subjective experience of pleasure is not a sufficient criterion for the value of certain behavior in terms of human happiness" (*Escape From Freedom*, 267).

7.

BUT IS IT SCRIPTURAL?

If it is true that people live according to their wants and priorities, then we should expect the Bible to reflect that idea in its teaching. The Bible never says in so many words, "Get your priorities straight," but I hope to show that the idea is one of its pervasive themes.

It does talk a lot about our wants—usually with the words *desires, pleasures, lusts,* or *passions,* and usually in a rather unflattering tone. The word lurking behind them all is *sin.*

James is particularly blunt. He has little use for the notion that we are passive instruments of sin, that it just somehow does itself through us while we look on piously perplexed.[1] James says, in effect, "We like to sin. That's why we do it so much." His words are: "Each one is tempted when he is carried away and enticed by his own lust. Then when lust has conceived, it gives birth to sin" (James 1:14–15). He then goes on to say, "What is the source of quarrels and conflicts among you? Is not the source your pleasures that wage war in your members? . . . You ask and do not receive, because you ask with wrong motives, so that you may spend it on your pleasures" (James 4:1, 3).

Let us not self-righteously kid ourselves: we love to sin. However willing the spirit might be, the flesh is still weak. Jesus says, "From within, out of the heart of men, proceed the evil thoughts and fornications [and other sins]" (Mark 7:21). Jude talks about "mockers, following after their own ungodly lusts" (Jude 18), and Peter talks about people with "eyes full of adultery" who "entice by fleshly desires" (2 Peter 2:14, 18; see also 1:4).

The heart of our spiritual problem is not what we do or

don't do, but what we want. The idea is right there in the Ten Commandments: Thou shalt not covet (commandment #10); don't covet your neighbor's things lest you steal (#8); don't covet your neighbor's wife or maid lest you commit adultery (#7); and, according to Colossians 3:5, greed amounts to idolatry (#2).

Despite the fact that the commandments address our wants, Paul makes it clear that rules and teachings "are of no value against fleshly indulgence" (Col. 2:23). Why? Because they don't do anything to change our *desire* to indulge the flesh. If anything, they arouse it.[2] And even if in obedience to a law or a teaching we refrain from carrying out the act, we earn no points with God because the sin consists in the underlying— though repressed—desire.[3]

The Bible presupposes that we have the capacity to choose, that we do make choices, and that we tend to make bad ones. People reject God not because some mystical force prevents them from accepting Him, but because they don't want Him: "O Jerusalem, Jerusalem, who kills the prophets and stones those who are sent to her! How often I wanted to gather your children together, the way a hen gathers her chicks under her wings, and you were unwilling" (Matt. 23:37; see also Ezek. 33:11). God gave us the capacity to choose and presents us with the choice: "I have set before you life and death, the blessing and the curse. So choose life in order that you may live" (Deut. 30:19). He also honors the choices we make—good and bad, wise and foolish—by granting us the consequences of them.

If we are slaves to sin, therefore, it is only because we have voluntarily chosen that master: "Do you not know that when you present yourselves to someone as slaves for obedience, you are slaves of the one whom you obey, either of sin resulting in death, or of obedience resulting in righteousness?" (Rom. 6:16). It's our choice. You need not "let sin reign in your mortal body that you should obey its lusts" (Rom. 6:12). We do it because we chronically want to.

HIGHER PRIORITIES

We can change or eliminate wants less readily than we can change or eliminate priorities. This is why I'll be talking about getting priorities straight rather than wants. Often it's impossible to get rid of a want; sometimes unhealthy. For instance, sex is a legitimate want, and it would be unhealthy to try to repress or get rid of it. Rather, it must be managed by higher priorities, such as faithfulness to one's spouse.

The idea of managing wants by higher priorities is an important biblical principle. Paul says, "Flee from youthful lusts, and pursue righteousness, faith, love and peace" (2 Tim. 2:22).[4] By choosing one thing, you automatically neglect something else. By reading this book, you're not mopping the floor. By becoming a postal clerk you incidentally exclude a career as a dentist or a circus barker. By walking in the Spirit, you incidentally neglect to fulfill the lusts of the flesh. By being kind to one another, you preclude being malicious to one another. By setting your mind on whatever is true, right, pure, and excellent, you leave little quarter for whatever is sinful and unholy.[5]

Over and over the Bible says, in effect, "Get your priorities straight!" That was one of Jesus' main themes, and He did not consider it a decision to be made lightly. Once, at a time when throngs were following Him, He turned around and threw the message in their faces like cold water: "If anyone comes to Me, and does not hate his own father and mother and wife and children and brothers and sisters, yes, and even his own life, he cannot be My disciple" (Luke 14:26–27). In other words, Don't imagine that you can blithely *add* Me to your life, be seen in My company, and come along when it's quite convenient. I come first or I don't come at all.

Count the costs, He continued; you wouldn't start to build a tower without first determining whether you can complete it. Nor would a king set out for battle without first determining whether he is really up to it. Neither should we glibly call Jesus Lord unless we have really thought through the implications of *making* Him lord. If we make Him first, that decision will have profound impact on every other decision we make in every nook and cranny of our lives.

One of the most familiar of Jesus' get-your-priorities-straight statements is in His Sermon on the Mount, "Seek ye first the kingdom of God, and his righteousness, and all these things shall be added unto you" (Matt. 6:33 KJV). Familiarity has worn smooth the keen edge of His meaning, so we tend to leave it as just a nice, sterile sentiment embroidered with lilies of the field and suitable for framing. How precious. But His context is the idea that you can't serve two masters and must therefore make a hard choice: Are you going to devote your energy to worrying about food and drink and clothing—and ministries and grades and clean carpets—or are you going to devote that energy to the first priority?[6] You can't serve two masters, so make up your mind which it's going to be! Seek out those areas of your life not yet submitted to His kingship, those in which He is not yet lord, and make Him lord over them. That's what seeking His kingdom means. It may be more exciting to devote your energies to spiritual gifts, healing, prophecy, doctrines, social causes, and the like, but the first priority must be making the Lord lord.

Not that there's anything wrong with such things, in their place, which is subject to His lordship. But as Augustine once said, "God wants to give us something, but cannot, because our hands are full—there's nowhere for Him to put it."[7]

THE HARDEST CORE OF JESUS' TEACHING

Jesus' theme of getting priorities straight is not just an occasional topic. He comes back to it time and time again. When He was visiting Mary and Martha, Mary sat calmly listening to what He had to say. Martha was busy trying to get lunch ready and working up a nasty resentment at the sight of Mary doing nothing but listening. When Martha finally exploded, "Lord, do You not care that my sister has left me to do all the serving alone? Then tell her to help me." Jesus told her to get her priorities straight: "Martha, Martha, you are worried and bothered about so many things; but only a few things are necessary, really only one, for Mary has chosen the good part" (Luke 10:38–42).

In Matthew 23 Jesus bawls out over and over, "Woe to you, scribes and Pharisees, hypocrites." Half of the times it is to attack their cockeyed priorities: the temple, Jesus says, is more important than the gold in it; the altar more important than the sacrifice on it; justice and mercy and faithfulness more important than tithes; inner cleanliness more important than outer cleanliness; and inner life more important than outside appearances.

In the parable of the sower, He talks about thorny ground on which the seed of the Word is sown, but "the worry of the world, and the deceitfulness of riches choke the word, and it becomes unfruitful" (Matt. 13:22). When a rich young man asked Jesus what he should do to obtain eternal life, Jesus first told him to obey the commandments, and rattled off a few. But when the man said he already did obey the commandments, Jesus sliced straight to his priorities: "One thing you lack: go and sell all you possess, and give it to the poor, and you shall have treasure in heaven; and come, follow Me" (Mark 10:17–22). Jesus was pulling the rug out from under the man's highest priority in life, and the man slunk away in despair.

In the Sermon on the Mount, Jesus repeatedly compares two values and shows which is the more important. He says, "Do not lay up for yourselves treasures upon earth, . . . but lay up for yourselves treasures in heaven; . . . for where your treasure is, there will your heart be also" (Matt. 6:19–21). As long as your treasure is on earth, it doesn't matter whether that treasure is wealth, people's approval, your career, your political party, or your house. Whatever has your heart—whatever you value above all else—is your treasure.

It is also liable to be your master, which is why Jesus' very next point is that you can't serve two masters and must therefore choose whether you're going to worry about material things or seek first the kingship of God. The rich young man's treasure—and master—was his wealth. Jesus therefore told him to get rid of it, "and you shall have treasure in heaven."

Jesus' point was not that selling off your furniture is a spiritual panacea, but that your treasure on earth—whatever it is—must go if it is taking precedence over Christ. As Robert Geulich says, "To have one's *treasure in heaven* means to submit oneself totally to that which is *in heaven—God's sovereign rule*" (*The Sermon on the Mount*, 328; italics his).

Jesus weaves all these threads together in two sublimely simple parables. "The kingdom of heaven is like a treasure hidden in the field, which a man found and hid; and from joy over it he goes and sells all that he has, and buys that field. Again, the kingdom of heaven is like a merchant seeking fine pearls, and upon finding one pearl of great value, he went and sold all that he had, and bought it" (Matt. 13:44–46).

The treasure, the pearl, takes precedence over every other consideration. The man reorders his priorities around the most important thing. Whatever else he has held dear suddenly loses its intrinsic appeal and becomes valuable to him only insofar as he can invest it toward the greater treasure. Whatever he might hold back would be just enough to prevent him from possessing the most valuable thing of all. He knows what matters and what doesn't. He invests all he has in the treasure because it is genuinely important enough to him. He wants to.

The kind of statements that represent the hardest core of Jesus' teaching, the ones that demand the most of us, are precisely the ones that call for us to get our priorities straight.

PAUL'S PRIORITIES

Like the man in the parables, Paul had his priorities sharply drawn—not because he had things ranked number six, seven, and eight, but because he was clear on number one. The book of Philippians, particularly chapter 3, is Paul's great statement of his priorities. "Whatever things were gain to me, those things I have counted as loss for the sake of Christ. More than that, I count all things to be loss in view of the surpassing value of knowing Christ Jesus my Lord, for whom I have suffered the loss of all things, and count them but rubbish in order that I may gain Christ" (Phil. 3:7–8).

Among the "all things" Paul counted as rubbish (literally, *manure*) compared with Christ was his very life: "Christ shall even now, as always, be exalted in my body, whether by life or by death. For to me, to live is Christ, and to die is gain. . . . I do not know which to choose. But I am hard-pressed from both directions, having the desire to depart and be with Christ, for that is very much better; yet to remain on in the flesh is more necessary for your sake" (Phil. 1:20–24).

He has no complaints about staying alive so he can continue ministering, but considers it much better to be with the Lord. Given that attitude, peripheral issues don't matter much. He can take them in stride. What's the worst thing that could happen to him? Be killed? Big deal! He'd rather be with the Lord anyway!

In our loyalties, time, attention, and actions, Jesus demands that we get our priorities straight. It's a dominant theme in the Bible precisely because it gets at the heart of how people operate.[8] Because we make our decisions according to either of two criteria—what we want or what is most important to us—they are the key to our behavior. Our wants and particularly our priorities are therefore what God homes in on. We make Him lord of our lives by making him our highest personal priority; then He can bring us and every lower priority under new management. His management.

NOTES

1. That notion goes back to a misapplication of Romans 7.

2. Romans 7:7. This is why, for example, it is often unwise to forbid your teenager to date someone of whom you disapprove. Forbidding it does nothing to change the desire to date that person, and more often than not

only intensifies that desire. Worse, it often puts the teenager into the position of choosing between you and that person.

3. Matthew 5:21–22, 27–28.

4. See also 1 Timothy 6:11 and Titus 2:11–12.

5. Galatians 5:16; Ephesians 4:29–32; Philippians 4:8. See also Colossians 3:2. Since thinking about one thing precludes thinking about something else at the same time, Paul says to make it your personal priority to give over your attention to whatever is true, honorable, right, and pure. He illustrates the same idea (only in terms of action rather than thoughts) elsewhere when he says, "No soldier in active service entangles himself in the affairs of everyday life, so that he may please the one who enlisted him as a soldier" (2 Tim. 2:4). You can't do both, he says, so do the one that is more important.

6. Robert Geulich's translation gets at the heart of Jesus' point: "Rather above all else seek his sovereign rule and righteousness" (*The Sermon on the Mount*, 322).

7. Cited in C. S. Lewis' *The Problem of Pain*, 96. The very first of the Ten Commandments establishes that the Lord is to be our first priority: "You shall have no other gods before Me" (Exod. 20:3; see also Col. 1:18 and Rom. 14:9). Anything that comes before Him—your family, ministry, job, home, happiness, plans—is an idol. Our commitment is to be to Christ Himself, not primarily to our local church or any religious leader, not even to the Bible. Even they can become substitutes for the real thing.

8. It is a pervasive theme. I won't claim that it's exclusive of all others, or the single most important, or even that it's entirely consistent with all others.

8. HOW GOD OPERATES

We have talked a good bit in earlier chapters about how God does *not* normally operate. Now let's talk about how He normally does.

The first thing to realize about how God normally operates is that He does His work in people through His Holy Spirit. The single most comprehensive explanation of the Holy Spirit's job is the one Jesus gives in John 14–16. Here are the kinds of things He says the Holy Spirit is in the business of doing:

> comfort us (14:16 KJV; Acts 9:31)
> be with us forever, abide in us, be in us (14:16–17)
> teach us all things (14:26)
> remind us of all that Jesus said (14:26)
> bear witness of Jesus, as will we (15:26–27)
> convict the world of sin, of righteousness, and of judgment (16:8–11)
> guide us into all truth (16:13)
> disclose what is to come (16:13)
> glorify Jesus, for He takes what is Christ's and discloses it (16:14)

Many of the other biblical statements of the Holy Spirit's jobs elaborate on these. Here are some others:

> inspire prophecy, dreams, visions (Joel 2:28)
> empower us (Acts 1:8; Luke 24:49)
> strengthen the inner person (Eph. 3:16)
> effect power, love, sound mind (2 Tim. 1:7)
> regenerate us (John 3:5–6)
> give life (John 6:63; Rom. 8:11)
> liberate us (2 Cor. 3:17)

fill us (Eph. 5:18)

shed God's love in us (Rom. 5:5)

lead us (Rom. 8:14)

witness that we are sons of God (Rom. 8:14)

assure us that we dwell in God (1 John 4:13)

intercede for us in prayer (Rom. 8:26–27)

teach us (1 Cor. 2:13)

wash, sanctify, justify us (1 Cor. 6:11)

produce fruit in us: love, joy, peace, patience, kindness, goodness, faithfulness, gentleness, self-control (Gal. 5:22–23)

give us gifts: wisdom, the word of knowledge, faith, healing, working miracles, prophecy, discerning spirits, tongues, interpretation of tongues (1 Cor. 12:8–10); service, teaching, exhortation, liberality, leadership, mercy (Rom. 12:6–8)

This list may not be exhaustive, but certain patterns do emerge. First, the Holy Spirit does His work inside us, in what we are and what we become. Second, He changes us, and outward manifestations are of that inward work. Third, He does what He does with us *as believers* (that is, He doesn't make you a better plumber—He makes you a better Christian). As an incidental side-effect of becoming a better Christian, you may become a better parent or roommate or citizen (because those are expressions of becoming a better person), but you won't become a better pianist or mathematician. That doesn't mean God doesn't care what you do for a living or a hobby, only that He is not in the business of developing your secular skills, much less of conducting your secular affairs on your behalf.

Central to the way the Lord does His job in us is that He enables us to understand the Word. After His resurrection, Jesus "opened [His disciples'] minds to understand the Scriptures" (Luke 24:45). God opened Lydia's heart to respond to Paul's words. Paul wrote that "whenever Moses is read, a veil lies over their heart; but whenever a man turns to the Lord, the veil is taken away" (2 Cor. 3:15–16). Conversely, a hardened heart will keep one from learning the Lord's lessons, and Satan blinds the minds of unbelievers from seeing the light of the gospel.[1]

PLANTING IDEAS

The Holy Spirit also works in us by inspiring ideas and words. Jesus told His disciples that the time would come when religious and civil authorities would drag them in for questioning: "The Holy Spirit will teach you in that very hour what you ought to say" (Luke 12:12). Don't even bother preparing a defense, He told them, "for I will give you utterance and wisdom which none of your opponents will be able to resist or refute" (Luke 21:15). In such a case, "it is not you who speak, but it is the Spirit of your Father who speaks in you" (Matt. 10:20).

Jesus exemplified this principle. He said, "The Father is in Me[.] The words that I say to you I do not speak on My own initiative, but the Father abiding in Me does His works" (John 14:10). Jesus was willing to allow the Father to use Him. Paul recognized that, while the principles of Jesus' life applied to him as a believer, he was far from the perfect exemplar of them that Jesus was. So he asked for prayer "that utterance may be given to me in the opening of my mouth, to make known with boldness the mystery of the gospel, . . . that in proclaiming it I may speak boldly, as I ought to speak" (Eph. 6:19–20).

God certainly does not inspire *all* ideas and words, but inspiring them is in His normal repertoire.

Nor does inspiration mean compulsion. God may well plant an idea in your head, but it is up to you to act on the idea or ignore it. It would be psychic rape for God to force you to go along with Him, but planting ideas in your head and emotions in your heart is certainly fair game. Advertisers plant ideas constantly. So do professors. Your boss does it; the president does it whenever he gives a speech; I'm doing it by writing this book. The difference is that God uses different means of planting and the content of His inspirations is quite different. But once planted, His inspirations must compete for your attention and cooperation on precisely the same basis as all the other ideas in your head: you choose.

What kinds of ideas will God plant? Take John 14–16 as a starting point. There Jesus said the Holy Spirit will "bring to your remembrance all that I said to you" (John 14:26). It seems fair to gather from the Bible that God inspires our imagination and creativity and brings things to our attention. But all New Testament references to God inspiring ideas or words relate directly to the spread of the gospel. When, for example, Jesus promised to give the disciples words when they got arrested, the purpose was not to help them sweet-talk their way out of custody: a hearing was to be "an opportunity for your testimony" (Luke 21:13).

Is God inspiring you to go into this store or make that phone call? Probably not. But He certainly is inspiring you to seek first His kingdom and to love your neighbor. You may feel that God is inspiring you to do or say this or that, but the more distant the relation of that idea to the gospel or godliness, the thinner your scriptural basis for attributing the idea to God.

CHANGING YOUR INNER ESSENCE

The Holy Spirit's work goes beyond the realm of ideas and words. Whatever Christian virtues God's people possess are His doing. He gives understanding, enlightenment, and a spirit of wisdom and of revelation.[2] He is the source of love and the one who causes it to increase in us; in a very real sense, He loves through us.[3] He is the giver of life, the author of faith, and the source of righteousness.[4]

God gives us all these things, but in a deeper sense He *is* all these things. He not only gives us peace, He *is* our peace. He not only gives us love and life, He *is* love and life. Likewise, He is our strength and help; power and wisdom; righteousness, sanctification, and redemption.[5] To ask Him to supply you with such things, therefore, is to ask for more of Him. You have them only if you have *Him*. And if you have Him in you, then you have *them* latent in you, whether you are taking advantage of them yet or not.

Of the ways God operates, none is more central to the principles of this book than this: God changes the inner essence of what you are. And these changes express themselves as changes in what you want and what is important to you. David prayed, "Create in me a pure heart, O God, and renew a steadfast spirit within me," and that is exactly what God is primarily in the business of doing (Psalm 51:10 NIV). All else is preparation or elaboration. God says, "I will give you a new heart and put a new spirit within you; and I will remove the heart of stone from your flesh and give you a heart of flesh" (Ezek. 36:26).

For God to give you a new heart is to give you *His* heart, to make you a new creature, born again, in the process of becoming conformed to the image of Christ. As the new displaces the old—and to the extent that you allow it to—you will increasingly want what God wants. What is important to Him will become important to you. "Those who live according to the sinful nature have their minds set on what that nature desires; but those who live in accordance with the Spirit have their minds set on what the Spirit desires" (Rom. 8:5 NIV).

AGREEING WITH GOD

You will, in short, come to agree with God. One of the most revealing statements in the Bible is, "God loves a cheerful giver" (2 Cor. 9:7). About the only time we ever hear that is just before the offering plate is passed, but it is a principle whose implications are far-reaching and profound. God could easily shake you by the ankles until all your money fell out, but instead He loves a cheerful giver. Why? Because a cheerful giver agrees with God! He or she wants what God wants: to give! A cheerful giver is one with no sense of reluctance or obligation or pretense, but a genuine, simple, sincere desire to give.

If *you* want to give, you *will* give. If you don't want to but think you should, you may or may not come through—but it won't matter either way because you won't be cheerful about it. You either do the will of God "from the heart" or you haven't done it at all (Eph. 6:6).

What matters is what we want and what is important to us. Sin doesn't happen to us; we do the sinning and we do it because we want to. But God is in the business of gradually replacing our desires to sin with desires to obey Him, to live a holy life, and to do what we should be doing. As J. B. Phillips says, "The whole point of real Christianity lies not in interference with the human power to choose but in producing a willing consent to choose good rather than evil."[6]

He'll change your wants from the inside out, but only by your permission. At each turn you have the right to say, in effect, "No, I'm not quite finished with that one yet." But countless Christians have found that they no longer want to do the things they used to dive into whole hog. They have begun to live, as Peter says, "no longer for the lusts of men, but for the will of God" (1 Peter 4:2). It's significant that Peter also says, "Do not be *conformed* to [your] former lusts" (1 Peter 1:14). Our wants define us. What we are expresses itself as what we value.

All this doesn't happen at the moment you become saved, of course. Replacing your wants with God's wants is a gradual, lifelong process. You won't ask, seek, or knock for anything unless you really want it enough to go to the trouble.

YOUR HEART'S DESIRE

There are two remarkable promises related to the idea of God's wants becoming yours. The first is from David: "Delight yourself in the LORD; and He will give you the desires of your heart" (Psalm 37:4). The second, from Jesus, is like it: "If you abide in Me, and My words abide in you, ask whatever you wish, and it shall be done for you" (John 15:7). Both promise, in effect, that God will give you whatever you want. Not bad.

But there's a catch: both the promises apply only if you delight yourself in the Lord, if you abide in Christ and His words abide in you. Well, if you *delight* yourself in the Lord, what kinds of things are likely to be the *desires* of your heart? Fame and fortune? If so, then your delight is not first in the Lord, but in the world. If, however, you delight in the Lord, your desire will be the Lord and the things of the Lord. Your desire will be to know Him, to enjoy His presence, to live His life, to be His person. And if those sorts of things are your desire, you have His promise to give them to you.

As you abide in Him and His words abide in you, you will be changed. And as you begin to want what God wants, you can pray for what you desire, because you will be praying for what *He* desires. You will be praying in His name. "It is God who is at work in you, both to *will* and to work for His good pleasure" (Phil. 2:13). He changes your work by changing your will. If you *will* for His good pleasure (that is, delight yourself in the Lord), you will *work* for His good pleasure—because it will now be your good pleasure too. The Lord will "direct your hearts into the love of God and into the steadfastness of Christ" (2 Thess. 3:5), and you can say with David, "I desire to do your will, O my God; your law is within my heart" (Psalm 40:8 NIV).

On this, Martin Luther is in complete agreement. "When God works in us," he says, "the will is changed under the sweet influence of the Spirit of God. It desires and acts not from compulsion, but responsively of its own desire and inclination. It . . . goes on to desire, crave after and love that which is good, just as once it desired, craved after and loved evil" (*Erasmus-Luther*, 111–12).

God's policy is reflected in the attitude Paul expressed to Philemon: Paul wanted to keep Philemon's runaway slave Onesimus with him, "but without your consent I did not want to do anything, that your goodness should not be as it were by compulsion, but of your own free will" (Philem. 13–14).

SELF-CONTROL

Did you ever notice that the final thing Paul lists as part of the fruit of the Spirit in Galatians 5:22–23 is self-control? Doesn't that strike you as a little bit odd? *Self*-control as part of the fruit of the Spirit?

Self-control makes no sense in that context if you think of it as merely restraining your behavior. The want is still there. Holding behavior in check would be of little value as long as the desire to do nasty things remains.[7] Stopping is certainly the first step in becoming free of the desire (as in smoking, fornicating, swearing, cheating, and so on), but only the first step. If all you ever do is stop doing something bad without replacing the desire to do it with a godly value, then your carnal achievement will easily become a source of self-righteousness, an exercise in legalism. God is less interested in what you don't do than in where your treasure is.

Self-control is far more radical than inhibiting behavior. To control yourself is to control your wants; specifically, to manage, overrule, and supplant your ungodly wants (which will still be there) with godly priorities.[8] On the one hand, we have instructions to change this and that desire;[9] on the other hand, we have the principle that God through His Spirit is doing the work in us. Which is it? Both! He does the replacing, but only if, where, and to the extent that we yield. To say *stop wanting to get drunk*, for instance, is to say *let God replace or overrule your desire to get drunk with one of His desires.*

If self-control is part of the fruit of the Spirit and if you have the Spirit, then you have self-control (along with all the other aspects) sitting latent in you, waiting to be exercised. You exercise it in practice by recognizing an unworthy desire as it crops up and overruling it with a godly value. Though it is not something you drum up carnally, it is a matter of practice: "The mature, . . . because of practice have their senses trained to discern good and evil" (Heb. 5:14).

In sum, God does His work *in* us, through the Holy Spirit. He enables us to understand the Scriptures and inspires words and ideas (principally those related to the gospel). He develops virtues in us, but those virtues are only expressions of what He Himself *is* in us.

Most important, for present purposes, He changes what we are from the inside out, replacing (to the extent we allow Him to) our old wants and priorities with His wants and priorities so that we come to agree with Him. When we agree with Him in our wants and priorities, we do His will because it has become our own will. Our obedience is only as good as our cheerful agreement with Him. Self-control, part of the fruit of the Spirit, is a matter of replacing or overruling our carnal wants and priorities with His.

NOTES

1. Acts 16:14; Mark 6:52; 2 Corinthians 4:4.

2. 2 Timothy 2:7; Ephesians 1:16–18. These are not just for their own sakes; rather, Jesus "has given us understanding, *in order that* we might know Him" (1 John 5:20).

3. 1 John 4:7–8; 1 Thessalonians 3:12–13; Philippians 1:8.

4. 1 Timothy 6:13; Hebrews 12:2; Philippians 3:9. It is particularly important to remember that righteousness originates in Him, lest we become self-righteous.

5. Ephesians 2:14; 1 John 4:8; Colossians 3:4; Psalm 46:1; 1 Corinthians 1:24, 30.

6. *God Our Contemporary* (New York: The Macmillan Company, First Macmillan Paperbacks ed., 1960), 89.

7. Matthew 5:21–28.

8. Paul says that God has given us the spirit "of power, and of love, and of a sound mind" (2 Tim. 1:7 KJV). It's interesting that the same word translated "sound mind" here is alternately translated *self-discipline* (NEB) and *sound judgment* (NASB margin). The Greek word means, literally, "wise discretion" (Thomas Newberry, *The Englishman's Greek New Testament*, 548).

9. 2 Timothy 2:22; 1 Corinthians 10:6; and others.

9. GOD IN YOU

Beethoven was not a genius because he wrote great music. He wrote great music because he was a genius. I am not a thief because I steal. I steal because I am a thief. One of the themes Jesus stressed over and over was that what we do is only an expression of what we are. This is why Jesus insisted that people must get their heart right, and why He never laid down a code of laws.

Jesus expressed the principle often and in various ways, but perhaps never more bluntly than this: "That which proceeds out of the man, that is what defiles the man. For from within, out of the heart of men, proceed the evil thoughts and fornications, thefts, murders, adulteries, deeds of coveting and wickedness, as well as deceit, sensuality, envy, slander, pride and foolishness. All these evil things proceed from within and defile the man" (Mark 7:20–23). He was talking there about bad things, but the principle applies to good things as well: "There is no good tree which produces bad fruit; nor, on the other hand, a bad tree which produces good fruit. For each tree is known by its own fruit. For men do not gather figs from thorns, nor do they pick grapes from a briar bush. The good man out of the good treasure of his heart brings forth what is good; and the evil man out of the evil treasure brings forth what is evil; for his mouth speaks from that which fills his heart" (Luke 6:43–45).

God looks on the heart—the inner being as expressed in what we want and what's important to us. In the Sermon on the Mount, Jesus illustrated the point by saying that adultery, for instance, is committed on a level deeper than action: lust. Likewise, murder is committed on a level deeper than action: anger.[1]

In the mechanics of how people operate, what we are does not express itself *immediately* in what we do. Specifically, what we are expresses itself in what we want and what is important to us. Those wants and priorities in turn express themselves in what we do. If, therefore, you *are* a perfectionist, you will probably *want* a tidy house and will *do* things to keep it that way. If you are nosey, you will want to know what your co-workers are up to and will tend to look at the papers on their desks. If you are conscientious, it will be important to you to do your duty and fulfill expectations, so you will tend to show up for engagements you would like to skip.

MISAPPLYING THE PRINCIPLE

The principle that what we *do* reflects what we *are* is sound and widely recognized. It can be misapplied, though, in several ways.

First, the principle is useful in broad strokes, but not in detail. I may leave messes because I am a slob, but my tendency to cut my meat one chunk at a time rather than all at once probably does not say much about my deep inner being.

Second, a given act may spring from any number of motives, a fact that makes quick analysis not always possible. My act of dropping money in the collection plate may derive from a sincere giving spirit, from guilt, from perceived social pressure, pride, conformity, or the desire for a tax deduction. This, no doubt, is why God looks on the heart rather than the act, and why Jesus says not to judge others.

Third, while there is merit in the conventional wisdom that a person's true self comes out in a crisis, a surprise, or an upset, it can also be a cruel oversimplification. It is probably a mistake to watch someone do something atypical and think, "Aha! Now his true self comes out!" An upset may reveal a usually concealed *aspect* of what someone is, but to say that this freshly turned soil is *the* true self is rather simplistic. Any behavior a person exhibits eighty percent of the time is bound to derive from some powerful aspect of that person's inner being—maybe not the aspect we think, but some aspect.

The most hypocritical people express an aspect of their real selves in their very hypocrisy. The aspect the Pharisees expressed may not have been piety—perhaps it was vanity or arrogance or a need to be noticed and admired—but it was genuine and deep-seated.

THE DIRTY WELL

While we can fool one another about what we really are and about our true motives, we certainly don't fool God. He slices through the contradictory things we do and zeroes in on the heart. What He sees is a jumble of contradictions, thrashing about in a soup we could call the sin instinct. Rather than fish out the contradictions piecemeal, though, He deals with the whole bowl of soup. As Ian Thomas says, " 'Sin' . . . has to do with what a man *is;* whereas 'sins' have to do with what a man *does.* . . . A person may be called upon a hundred times to face the lesser issues of what he has done, without once being confronted with the greater issue of what he is" (*The Mystery of Godliness,* 11–12; italics his). Sin, says Thomas, is the cause, and sins are the effect. "*Sin* is the dirty well, *sins* are the dirty water! . . . It is . . . possible to keep the dirty water inside the dirty well, but this does not make the well clean!" (*The Mystery of Godliness,* 91; italics his).

Being good in order to counteract our sin instinct is like scrubbing in the shower to get rid of a sun tan. We must be changed from the inside out: born again, made new creatures. That sin instinct must be overpowered by a new, spiritual instinct.

The only way to get such a spiritual instinct is by having the Holy Spirit introduced into our inner being. God's great mystery, hidden for ages but now revealed, is precisely that: "Christ *in* you, the hope of glory" (Col. 1:25–27). This is what Christianity is all about: getting Him into you, establishing Him as Lord, and implementing His life-long program of conforming you into His image from the inside out. The only thing that counts is becoming a new creature.[2]

Well, what is the old creature? A person "is" the aggregate of his or her character, personality, temperament, genetic makeup, upbringing, experiences, attitudes, assumptions, fears, outlook, talents, imagination, and so on—dominated by a sin instinct.

Into this milieu God plants His Holy Spirit in the human spirit at the moment we "receive Christ." He enters only by your permission and He works only by your permission. Not all of the constituents of what you are can be changed, but He goes about changing those that can be and that need to be, to the extent that you allow Him to. He may need to change your identity so you think of yourself as a believer first and a businessperson or student or soldier or nice guy or parent second. When conflicts arise because of your various roles, the first can then take priority.

Paul explains how it works: "You lay aside the old self, which is being corrupted in accordance with the lusts of deceit, and . . . be renewed in the spirit of your mind, and put on the new self, which in the likeness of God has been created in righteousness and holiness of the truth" (Eph. 4:22–24). You "lay aside the old self" by allowing the Holy Spirit to overrule it. You don't have an accelerator in the process, only a clutch to engage and suspend the power and a brake to stop it completely.

It's easy to say we need to be born again since we have a sin instinct, but what about once we *have* been born again? How come we're still sinful? Simply because the renewal is an ongoing daily process.[3] We "lay aside" the old self and "consider [ourselves] . . . dead to immorality," (Col. 3:5), but the old self, the sin instinct, is still there. The most devoted Christian still sins as an expression of that residue. After all, is a devoted Christian a simple, one-dimensional, immaculate Adam with no thought ever of anything but God, His will, and His glory? Probably not. The most devoted Christian is born again, a new creature in Christ, yet one with a distinct and aggravating tug of war between the spirit and the flesh. (See Romans 7.)

God does not pump the dirty water out of our dirty wells all at once. Rather, He shines in His light to evaporate it. We remain entirely free to cover the well at any moment and block out the light. Even as the light shines, the deeper water takes longer to get rid of. And, of course, we all have a nasty habit of letting rain in to replenish the waters.

There is no biblical indication that we ever arrive in this life. Even Paul says flatly that he did not regard himself as having arrived.[4] But the purpose of God's work in us is never in doubt and never varies. He is in the process of making us into a "new self . . . in the likeness of God" (Eph. 4:24), a "new self . . . renewed . . . according to the image of the One who created" us (Col. 3:10), "conformed to the image of His Son" (Rom. 8:29). You may have lesser goals in mind, but God does not.

GOD'S WORKSHOP

Regardless how much or how little one matures, or how long it takes, the point is that God does His work in the inner person, the heart, what we are. As He changes what we are, our wants and priorities change accordingly. As our wants and priorities change we make different decisions, and our behavior changes accordingly.[5]

God's role in human affairs is therefore indirect: He changes what we are—the inner; we in turn change what we do—the outer. He does not normally work directly in what you and I do—nor, therefore, does He normally work directly in what *other* people do that affects us, that is, our circumstances! God's workshop is not our circumstances, but our innermost being. His method is not to act directly through our limp, available bodies or to work around people by making things happen. Rather, His method is to work through the Christian indirectly by changing what we are, and those changes express themselves as changed wants and priorities. We do God's will, we live the Christian life, and we share in the image of Christ when and to the extent that we agree with His wants and priorities, because they then are our own.

This is how Christ goes about living His life in and through us, the *body* of Christ, today. He is the cause; our behavior is the effect. It's not a case of manipulation or even of knee-jerk obedience, but of agreement. Ian Thomas likens the relation between God and your behavior to that between electricity and the light from a lamp: "You can enjoy the light," he says, "but you still cannot say that you have seen electricity! You can only say that you have seen a pure expression of it. In the same way, your behavior was intended by God to be a pure expression of His divine nature, though He remains unseen, and you can no more produce this effect *of yourself,* than a bulb can produce light of *itself!.* . . It is only the Spirit of God acting within you, who can ever enable you to behave as God intended you to behave!" (*The Mystery of Godliness,* 47; italics his).

How can you know whether your behavior is originating in the Holy Spirit or in yourself? By the fruit you bear. The fruit of the Spirit is love. The test is that simple.[6]

Just as God does His work in what we are rather than in what we do, so does He help us cope with our circumstances, not by changing them for us, but by supplying us with the inner resources we need. Armor is an external protection, but all the armor God supplies is internal: truth, righteousness, the gospel, faith, salvation, and His Word. He also supplies the inner power.[7] In the midst of a very practical, physical problem, Paul begged for relief, but God answered, "My *grace* is sufficient for you" (2 Cor. 12:9). We might often prefer a timely bolt of lightning to get rid of some problem, but God does not normally operate that way.

To expect God to tinker in your circumstances, therefore, is to miss the whole point of Christianity. Jesus offers no hope for this world; He only guarantees tribulation. I don't say that as a pessimist or as a fan of hellfire and brimstone. Those just happen to be the facts.[8] Our hope, peace, joy, and life are in Him. The hope He offers is for *inner* peace and *eternal* life. This world and everything in it—our homes, businesses, music, science, hairdos, circumstances—are passing.[9] Your inner being is what's going to last for eternity. So that's where God concentrates His attention.

MIRACLES IN THE WRONG PLACES

That's not where many of us concentrate our attention, though. One of the ironies of evangelical culture is that, while reading God's hand into your circumstances is considered a sure sign of spirituality, you need not be a born-again believer at all to develop that prized habit. In fact, reading His hand into circumstances can be an *evasion* of genuine commitment to being His person in them. It can be an insidious *alternative* to giving Him your heart—because it keeps your attention directed outward rather than inward, where His chisel bites.

Though Jesus stresses the inner rather than the outer, we tend not to follow His perspective through to its inevitable implications and applications. We have evolved a religion of coincidences, in which we can read God's hand into everything that "happens"—the outer—without ever allowing Him to make us new creatures.[10] We can routinely ask God to intervene in our circumstances while hoping He'll keep His nose out of inner things like our spiritual indifference and pride.[11]

It's a sublimely easy mistake to make. But we seek miracles in the wrong places when we make it. God does not abandon us to grope around on our own the best we can, but neither is He beside us cleaning up our messes.[12] He is inside us cleaning up *us!*

NOTES

1. Matthew 5:21–22, 27–28.

2. Galatians 6:15.

3. 2 Corinthians 4:16.

4. Philippians 3:13-14.

5. Even if I'm all wet about the intermediate stage of wants and priorities, God's work would still be one step removed from our behavior.

6. See 2 Corinthians 13:5; 1 John 4:12–16; John 15:4–5.

7. Ephesians 6:10, 13–17; 3:16.

8. John 16:33; 15:18–20; 2 Timothy 3:12.

9. 2 Peter 3:10.

10. Some people seem to believe more firmly in providence than they do in God. Jesus denounced the cities in which most of His miracles were performed, because, though they were wowed by the supernatural pyrotechnics, "they did not repent" (Matthew 11:20). It is more comfortable to look for God to open doors and give us signs than it is to let Him make radical changes in what we are.

11. According to Jesus, the important thing is not so much whether we know God, but whether He knows us (Matt. 7:23; Luke 13:25-27; see also 1 Cor. 8:3). What's the difference? Someone can get to know you only to the extent that you open up to them and give them access to your deepest parts. As God, He can of course pry in to see your heart, but knowing is something deeper than seeing. He wants us to *be willing* to bare it to Him. That means taking off our fig leaves and taking down our "Keep Out" signs.

12. It's our job as Christians to walk beside one another.

10.   A FEW SUBTLETIES

I realize that at first glance it seems like a hopelessly naïve oversimplification to account for the vast majority of human decisions in terms of wants and priorities. No doubt we can all think of plenty of things we do that we neither want nor that seem very important to us. Doesn't that invalidate the principle? No, because what we want and what is important to us may not be readily apparent or simple. So we need to look at some of the subtleties or complications of the principle.

MEANS TO ENDS

The first subtlety is that, while many of the things we choose to do are not *themselves* intrinsically valued, we do them because they are means to some ends that we *do* value.

From the mundane to the earth-shaking, most of what we do is a means to some end. The reason I scratch my nose is not simply that it itches, but that I want to make it *stop* itching—and scratching is a means to that end. The president sends in the troops as a means of accomplishing some military or diplomatic purpose. The doctor prescribes a certain medication as the means he or she considers best suited to the end of relieving the patient's sickness. I glance left while driving as a means of relieving the monotony of looking straight ahead.

In some cases we might not like the means much, but if the end is important enough to us, we will accept the means as the price of achieving the end. For instance, I once agreed to help a colleague set up tables for a weekend conference—at 7:30 Saturday morning. When the alarm went off at 5:30, I certainly didn't *want* to get up and go, nor was it important to me to set up tables. What was important to me, though, was to appear dependable. Keeping my promise was a means to that end, so I dragged out of bed and went.

Likewise, paying taxes is itself not anything I want to do, nor is it very high on my priorities. But avoiding a run-in with the IRS is a higher priority than keeping that tax money, so I pay up. A parent may hate to spank a child, but if investing in the child's long-term discipline takes priority over evading that task, the parent spanks.

Conversely, if the means is just so distasteful that we would rather forego the end than endure the means, we will. Some people are tax rebels: as a matter of principle, they would rather go to jail than pay. And they do. Some medical students give up their chances to become doctors by dropping out because they would rather not dissect a cadaver. I may want to obey Jesus' instruction to confront someone directly about a problem, but if I want to avoid the confrontation more than I want to resolve the problem, I will go with that stronger value and try to avoid the person or the subject.

We may let one valued end take priority over another valued end. I may want to scratch my nose to make it stop itching, but often I don't do so, perhaps because I don't want to drop the kettle of hot soup I'm carrying or don't want to appear undisciplined in polite company. On a larger scale, this dilemma of choosing between competing valued ends is all too familiar to people in important decision-making roles in business, government, and elsewhere. For instance, we want cars that are safe, but we also want them to get good gas mileage, so automakers strip metal out of their cars to reduce weight for fuel efficiency—which also reduces safety. They make their choices. Whichever end is a higher priority to the decision maker will elbow out the lower priority end.

In many such cases, arriving at a compromise between competing values may *itself* become the goal of the moment. We see that in countless committee meetings or when members of Congress face a choice between wrangling on forever over a given bill or adjourning for a scheduled recess. No one likes all the particulars of the final agreement, but accepting it is a means to the end they do want: to reach a compromise before their deadline.

A single means may of course serve several ends.[1] By voting for a certain bill, a senator may simultaneously satisfy important constituents, soothe his or her own conscience, get rid of a problem, and improve prospects for re-election. Likewise, there may be any number of different means of accomplishing the same end. By assuming you have to do one thing, you close off your option of accomplishing the same end by some other, more godly, more creative, more pleasant, perhaps even more effective means. Half the problems in life are solved by eliminating an assumption.

For example, four men once carried a palsied friend to a house where Jesus was teaching and healing. The place was so crowded, though, that they couldn't get him in the door. Most people would have given up and gone home. But these four realized there was more than one means to their goal, so they climbed onto the roof, tore out the tiles, and lowered their friend down. Jesus honored their faith—and their imagination—by healing their friend.

The idea of a means to an end is much the same as the idea of actions having consequences. *A* is a means to *B*. *A* results in *B*. I may not like the means but I put up with it as the price of reaching the end that I do want; or I may not like the consequences of what I do, but am stuck with them as the price of having done what I did want to do.

In short, we do what we want to do or what is most important to us—which often is not so much the act (the means) but the end in view.

The ends we value show up in our behavior in countless ways. Some men, for instance, choose to swelter in a suit jacket on a scorching day rather than break protocol by taking it off. Protocol is a higher priority end to them than comfort. Some people choose to turn in assignments late rather than compromise their perfectionism by curtailing their endless fussing with details. Perfection is a higher priority end to them than punctuality. We may be all but oblivious to how tenaciously we will cling to considerations like protocol, perfectionism, equilibrium, stability, security, convention, tradition, familiarity, convenience, niceness, politeness, timidity, comfort, living up to other people's expectations, maintaining a habit, upholding an image, staying out of the way, and so on.

This understanding of means to ends gives us a valuable insight into one of the critical principles Jesus drove home again and again. The one sin that got His blood boiling more than any other was not dishonesty or adultery or malice—but hypocrisy. That, of all things, was what He blasted the Pharisees for time after time.

Why? What was so bad about their hypocrisy? If we think of it as consisting merely in their teaching or pretending one thing while in fact practicing something contradictory, we will miss Jesus' main point. What He nailed them for was that they were using God and the things of God *as a means to some other end.* That's what was insidious about the Pharisees' example. "They do all their deeds *to be noticed* by men" (Matt. 23:5). That attention was what they valued, not God. "How can you believe, when you receive glory from one another, and you do not seek the glory that is from the one and only God?" (John 5:44). Theirs was a problem of priorities: their first priority was social status, to which end God was but a means. What greater affront to God could there be? Better to ignore Him altogether than to exploit Him as a means to something else you value more highly.

If attention and approval—or equilibrium or comfort or anything else—is the more important end to us, we will do all sorts of things that are means to that end. If, however, we are seeking first the kingdom of God, the things we do will be means to that end.

RISK

A second subtlety that can go unnoticed in making decisions according to our wants and priorities is the risk factor.

Often what we face is not a question of *sacrificing* one priority for another, but of *risking* one for another. We'll balance a glass of milk on the arm of the sofa; we don't *know* whether it will tip over or not, but we don't think it's likely to, so we choose the low risk of spilling, over the inconvenience of moving the glass to a more stable spot.

The principle is this: An option rises or sinks in our priorities according to the perceived likelihood of a good or bad outcome. And that's a matter of judgment. For example, staying alive is far more important to me than getting somewhere on time, yet I have often driven dangerously fast in order to make a class or a meeting. It's not that I prefer death and dismemberment over getting there late. It's that I consider it unlikely that I will have an accident this time. I am risking my life and health, but I perceive the risk of an accident to be smaller than that of being embarrassed for my tardiness. So I choose, in effect, punctuality over safety.

We cope with risk constantly. How likely is it that the colors of my new shirt will run if I wash it in warm water? Or that confronting so-and-so about a problem will solve it or aggravate it? Or that the Soviets will respond a certain way to the president's foreign policy moves? We can't answer such questions with certainty, so we estimate the risk.

There is an entire academic discipline of trying to quantify risk, studied by engineers, actuaries, psychologists, business-people, economists, philosophers, mathematicians, and others. They come up with elaborate formulae and equations to quantify, say, how likely a bridge is to collapse or a new product to get a certain market share in a certain amount of time.

But even the people who design those equations recognize that people don't make decisions that way in the moment to moment of real life.[2] Risk is an entirely subjective value. Even the mathematical equations are based on subjective estimates.

Different people perceive a given prospect as more or less risky, and the same person's perception of a risk will change with time and circumstances. People disagree in their guesses about a given event because some have more or less information than others, some forget relevant information, some are more optimistic or pessimistic by nature, their respective prior experiences give them different bases for their expectations, and some will believe data that others dismiss.[3]

Our probability estimates are always based on ignorance. That's why we *make* them—because we *don't* know the future. Nonetheless, we sometimes *expect* ourselves to ("Why didn't I realize that would happen?" "I should have been there at the critical moment").[4]

But any time we plan for or try to anticipate the future (which we do constantly), we estimate probabilities. We are often—perhaps usually—wrong, but that's the only way we can operate.

There are always risks, but we learn to work around them. Flying an airplane is risky business, but pilots do it all the time, even in bad weather. It is important to get passengers where they want to go, keep the airline in business, move the mails, and so on. The pilots and other airline people minimize the risks by rigorous training, backup copilots, and instruments. But there comes a point at which the risk becomes unacceptable and they ground the plane rather than try to take off or land in bad weather. At whatever point one considers any risk too great to take, that option plunges in priority: We choose playing it safe over risking it.

It's important to remember, though, that risk (or whatever word we use: probability, likelihood, chance, the odds) is not a real something. It's a belief about something, a seat-of-the-pants mathematical estimation. As mathematician Persi Diaconis says, "Probability is a property of a person, not of an object." It is not a cause of anything, nor a force influencing the outcome. It is merely an external, superimposed summary of other factors.

For example, the odds are heavily against any baseball team winning the World Series after losing the first two games at home. In the Series' entire eighty-two-year history, no team ever had—until 1985 when the Kansas City Royals did it. The odds said it was next to impossible. But the odds don't cause fielders to drop baseballs. If you let the odds of failure get you down, you're beaten already. Odds certainly won't help you succeed at anything, but *intimidation* by the odds will easily cripple you and help you fail.

In sum, none of us knows the future, yet we must continually make decisions based on what we believe about the future. We get a sense of the likelihood of this or that, and act accordingly. We may well be wrong in our risk assessment and suffer the consequences of our error, but that's life. Often the choice we face is not between a simple this or that, but between this and the *risk* of that. In such cases, the greater the risk we perceive, the lower that option will be in our priorities.

TIME

The third subtlety in the principle of wants and priorities is the time factor. In stating the principle originally, I was careful to say that we do what we want or what is most important to us "at the moment we make the decision." It's an important caveat. Priorities operate on both a broad life-policy scale and on a decision-by-decision scale, so they change from year to year, day to day, and moment to moment as our character, information, moods, and circumstances change.

Each decision, therefore, is like a snapshot of our wants and priorities at the moment the decision was made. Esau, for instance, traded his birthright to his brother, Jacob, for a bowl of stew at a moment when he was weak with hunger. He later regretted that decision, but at the moment he made it, food was more important to him: "I am about to die; so of what use then is the birthright to me?" (Gen. 25:27–34).

The way our priorities change with time may represent a healthy flexibility in responding to changing circumstances, or it may represent unprincipled wishy-washiness. Pontius Pilate, for example, knew full well that Jesus was innocent[5] and tried every maneuver he could think of to free Him. But as the charges of the priests and the chants of the mob drummed louder and louder in his skull, Pilate let other concerns take precedence over his own sense of justice: appeasing the priests and the mob, protecting his image as a tough guy, and avoiding Caesar's displeasure by allowing a disorderly crowd to claim that a king was competing with Caesar. Under the pressure of the moment, he buckled and he condemned Jesus. But then he quickly turned around and ordered a sign saying, "This is the king of the Jews," placed on the cross. It was suddenly very important to him to reassert his initiative and authority.

Herod did much the same thing. John the Baptist had been a pain in Herod's royal neck for insisting that he should not have his brother's wife, Herodius. He wanted to kill John, but was afraid of the people (who considered John a prophet), so he chose order over vengeance and just arrested him.

Herod's priorities changed on his birthday, though. Herodius' daughter so pleased Herod with her dance that he promised before all his dinner guests to give her anything she wanted. When she asked for John's head on a platter, Herod faced a dilemma: not only was he still concerned about order among the *people*, but he himself had come to recognize that John was a holy man. He had even taken a liking to him after all. "Yet because of his oaths and because of his dinner guests, he was unwilling to refuse her" (Mark 6:26).

So John died because Herod let his momentary concern for the way he looked in front of his dinner guests take priority over his more responsible concerns for civil order and for a man's life.

Time pressures do not necessarily bring out our "true" priorities, but they certainly do make us acutely conscious of the principle that we do what is most important to us at the moment. We'll cancel or postpone all sorts of other important things to get the tax return in the mail April 15. We'll let countless things slide when we need to take care of a sick child. Whether it's getting to a sale when the doors open, getting to the box office before the windows close, or even watching a favorite television show, we always manage to make time for the things that are genuinely important to us at the moment. Under time pressures it suddenly becomes much easier to say no to would-be conflicts.

Jesus is after the kind of commitment we have when our plane takes off at 2:15 and we order our whole day around the flight. That priority is settled, and we accommodate other things to the extent that they don't compromise that fixed intention.

Christianity requires a sobering level of maturity because, other than your death and Jesus' Second Coming, Christianity doesn't really *have* any deadlines. If you don't get around to reading the Bible today, you still can tomorrow—or the day after that. Or the day after that.

Death and the Second Coming aren't terribly pressing either. It's been two thousand years now, Jesus isn't back yet, and we don't honestly expect Him in the next day or so; nor do we really expect to die just yet. So we get lazy. And our priorities get scrambled. We settle for the most mundane and meaningless of priorities: just keeping up with whatever happens to be "going on" or is most urgent at the moment—the tyranny of the urgent. By habitual procrastination we let a world of other things take priority over our faith, and we lose any sense of direction to our lives. Small wonder life seems meaningless, even to many believers.

This, by the way, is one reason cults elicit such firm commitment from so many people: the followers have somebody to tell them what to do, when to do it, and how to do it. That security is very appealing to some people. But Christianity doesn't work very well as a religion because Jesus scrapped the whole apparatus of rules and regulations and religious bosses who would dish out assignments to keep us on track. Those make for orderly religion, but for immature believers.

In their place, Jesus insists on a personal relationship with each believer. No deadlines. No laws. No priesthood. Just the

Holy Spirit resident within us. Such a relationship takes maturity—but spiritual maturity is precisely what He is in the business of developing in us.

As we mature, we should learn to wield time wisely in making our decisions. Paul says, "Be careful how you walk, not as unwise men, but as wise, *making the most of your time*, because the days are evil" (Eph. 5:15–16).[6] Jesus, in explaining why it was okay for a woman to pour expensive oils on His head instead of selling them for the poor, said, "The poor you have with you always; but you do not always have Me" (Matt. 26:11). What we should concentrate on here is His logic: that it is wiser to take advantage of a fleeting opportunity while it is available—if it is a priority—than to pass it by for something you could do another time.[7]

If that sounds suspiciously like a rationale for the tyranny of the urgent, remember He assumes the fleeting opportunity is worth grabbing in the first place.

If your priorities are clear, you may discover that you have fewer things to do. By concentrating on the few important things, you will almost automatically jettison many unimportant though urgent things. They won't stick in your attention long enough to become a tough issue.

One final point: Time is life—nothing more, nothing less. The way you spend your hours and your days is the way you spend your life.

NOTES

1. And some things we do may be means to some deep psychological end of which we are unaware, such as punishing ourselves, fulfilling a neurotic craving, lashing out at someone. One of the main goals of psychologists and psychiatrists is helping people recognize the true ends to which much of their behavior is a means.

2. In his book on mathematical decision models *Making Decisions*, D. V. Lindley commends such methods as the rational way people *should* make decisions. But he writes, "It is a defect of formal scientific thinking of the

CIRCUMSTANCES

type used in this book that it does not include within the formalism any scope for originality or bright ideas. It is more the thinking of a computer than a human being" (166).

3. Some people are also less averse to risk than others, so they tend to take chances other people would not take. An additional factor may be involved in their cases, such as enjoyment of the risk itself.

4. It is as absurd as it is common for people to feel tremendous guilt over some unanticipated consequence of something they did, based on the false assumption that they *should* have known the consequences. A psychologist friend of mine tells me that guilt is the single most prominent cause of mental disorders. That's a needless tragedy, since guilt is precisely what God dealt with once and for all on the cross.

5. John 18:38.

6. See also Colossians 4:5 and Galatians 6:10.

7. See also John 9:4.

11.   GET YOUR PRIORITIES STRAIGHT

If it is true that a key biblical theme is to get your priorities straight, then how do we go about doing so? There's an easy answer, but it's not very useful. The deeper answer is less obvious, but ultimately more effective.

Priorities operate on the level of big-league, life-scale policies and also on the level of mundane, minute-by-minute preferences. Life-scale priorities involve things like God, family, career, honesty, health, social life. Mundane priorities involve things like answering the phone rather than dashing out the door, standing silent rather than answering back to a berating boss, saving money on a baby-sitter rather than getting away to spend quality time alone with your spouse.

The obvious way to get one's priorities straight is to sit down and seriously think through what should and what should not be important to you. Settling the big issues once and for all can be a valuable growth experience. It can settle a lot of smaller issues before they arise. But there are some serious practical limitations to the value of deciding priorities in the abstract.

First, you can't practically cope with (much less think of) all the things that might be important to you. Things like health, happiness, safety, security, being liked, respected, comfortable, or alive may all be important to you, but how can you meaningfully rank them? Which should be number five? And how would you rank prayer, sharing Christ, reading the Word, spending time with family, with friends, alone? All are important, but it would be pointless to try to list them in order of priority.

Second, settling your priorities once and for all in the

abstract works only to the extent that you apply that grand decision instance by instance in the little decisions of life. The one-time decision is a first step, and we all love first steps. They satisfy our urge for progress—which we can then do without after getting the first step out of our system. But first steps are of little use without consistent follow-up. In fact, they can be dangerous by lulling us into a false sense of accomplishment.

Jesus had little use for what preachers today call professions of faith, those one-time statements of commitment. Almost every time anybody blurted out something like, "I'll follow you anywhere," Jesus replied, in effect, "Oh, will you? Prove it." One-time decisions are cheap; Jesus insisted on commitment for the long haul—a commitment not to be made lightly.[1] If you don't apply the grand decision consistently in the small ones, it will remain just one isolated decision, whittled down to nothing by the swarm of abrasive contrary ones.

Priorities are determined, not at one fell swoop, but one decision at a time. Priorities set in the abstract have a nasty habit of shifting around when real choices arise. I may decide tonight that my first priority is going to be loving my neighbor, but next time I'm running late and see somebody's car broken down beside the road, I am quite likely to let concern for my busy schedule or perhaps my own safety elbow its way ahead of what I had thought was my first priority.

YOUR ACTUAL PRIORITIES

The moment is what counts, because that is when decisions are made. And just as minutes add up to years, so do all those little improvised decisions add up to sweeping patterns that reveal what our priorities really are. And our actual priorities may bear little resemblance to what we think they are or ought to be.

The most useful thing to do, then, is not to plan for the future, but to frankly assess your priorities as they stand now. Think back through the choices you've made lately. Don't worry about what you think they *ought* to be, just about what they are. How often have you chosen:

your job over your family?

your ministry over your personal walk with the Lord?

faraway impersonal political, moral, or other causes over people around you?

saving a little money over phoning a loved one?

impressing strangers over being true to loved ones' needs?

your own pride or comfort over other people's needs?

other people's opinions over your own principles?

your leisure time over your responsibilities (or vice versa)?

income over happiness?

the security of the familiar over the risk of failure on something new?

appearances over content?

hanging onto what you are over starting to become what you can be?

getting your way over helping make the project succeed?

What patterns emerge? What kinds of things tend to win? Which lose consistently?

If you think through such questions seriously, the answers will probably show you what your current priorities really are. Then ask yourself the most important question of all: Are you happy with the kinds of choices you've been making?

Reassessing your priorities need not mean reordering them. You may wind up reaffirming them. If you are satisfied with them as they stand, then the experience of reassessing them will have only strengthened you. A psychologist friend of mine, for example, wants to write a guidebook to the psyche, but has postponed the project indefinitely because of his family responsibilities. He's comfortable with that decision because he's clear on his priorities.

Nor are your various commitments and priorities necessarily in conflict with one another. It is important to me to earn a living and also important to do work that is interesting. I don't necessarily have to choose between the two; I can do both. If I were a physicist, for instance, my commitment to science need not be incompatible with my commitment to Christ: given a belief in God, science is simply a matter of discovering how His ingenious universe operates.

It's not for me to recommend conclusions you should reach. But I can say this: If you mean to let God play any role in your life at all, He won't settle for anything lower than first priority. Are you really willing to be God's person? Not do you think you *ought* to be, but do you *want* to be? If you don't, you won't be. And you are entirely free to say no. There are eternal consequences, but it's your decision.

If you do want to be God's person, are you honestly willing to make Him and His ways first priority? How often lately have you chosen Him over competing interests? Are you satisfied with your track record? Is He? In what things are you *not* yet willing to yield to Him? Why? What will it take for you to become willing?

Get those questions settled, then live out your settlement one decision at a time. If you do make the Lord first priority— that is, make the Lord lord—He will begin to take care of the other, lower priorities.

NOTES

1. Luke 14:25–35; 8:13; Matthew 8:19–20; 21:28–32; John 8:30–31; 16:30-32.

12.

THE PURPOSE(S)
OF LIFE

It's terribly impolite to ask anyone point blank what they believe is the purpose of life. Any thinking person is expected to ask the question rhetorically from time to time, but no one is really expected to have an answer, at least not on the tip of the tongue. Likewise, it is dangerous to give an answer confidently, because the tendency is to suppose that if anyone is simpleton enough to spell out the purpose of life, he or she can't possibly be right. So it must be something else.

We should be suspicious of packaged answers to such a fundamental question. But we should be equally suspicious of aimless asking that never aspires to an answer at all. So let's take the risk.

In this book we are discussing the mechanics of the Christian life and priorities. But clear priorities come from a clear sense of purpose and, besides, no mechanism makes much sense unless you know its purpose. By knowing the purpose our Creator has for us, we can make better sense of His Word, His will, and His workings in our lives, and can more intelligently respond by setting our priorities according to that purpose. Knowing our purpose is also the only basis for assessing whether or not we are working right.

One problem with talking about the purpose of life is that, I suspect, most people who ask rhetorically what it is don't really want to know. If you don't know and you find out, you must either change your life accordingly or come up with some rationalization for not doing so. Neither prospect is pleasant.

Nonetheless, I suspect most people do have some sense of a purpose of life, even if they can't articulate it, wouldn't use the word *purpose* to describe it, or don't live up to it very consistently. Their purpose may be as vague as "survive as best you can as long as you can" or "get by and keep from leaving too big a mess in your wake." Or it may be a bit more specific, like "raise children" or "get all the money and things you can before somebody else does."

A second problem with talking about the purpose of life is that many people want a *personal* answer: "Sure, that's fine for you, but what about me?" The underlying assumption is that there really is no overall purpose for human beings, so we each have to make one up to suit ourselves.

But the Bible does offer humankind's overall purpose, within which each person can dig out his or her own personal application. There is still, of course, a danger of oversimplification. It is best to say, then, that the Bible does not state one single purpose, but gives several, which all hover around a common ground.

JESUS' AND PAUL'S PURPOSES IN LIFE

Knowing what God wanted to accomplish in sending His Son to live and die on earth will tell us what is important to our Creator, which in turn will tell us a lot about His purposes for us. So will knowing what Paul said were his purposes. Then there are the more straightforward statements of our purposes: verses with phrases like "in order that . . ." or "that we might . . ." A collection of such verses makes up the appendix. Other verses may strongly imply purpose, but these are ones that state it rather unambiguously. Refer to the appendix for the details; here we'll look only at the patterns that emerge from those verses. We'll look at the various purposes given in Scripture, then see what they all add up to.

Jesus knew exactly what His purposes were. He stated them in a variety of ways, but He stated them over and over: "I came to do this," "God sent Me to be that." His own statements of His purpose and those of others about Him fall into a few categories:

1. He came to deal with sin and it's author, Satan, once and for all and to restore God's people to God.
2. He came to give us life—not just in the abstract, but through Himself.
3. He came to enlighten humankind, to preach God's truth, to be the light of the world—that we might know God.
4. He came to die, but only as the means to further ends:
   A. to deliver us from Satan, evil, and fear
   B. to establish His lordship
   C. to make us holy, righteous, pure, clean, blameless, and sanctified.

Out of Jesus' clear sense of purpose grew His clear sense of priorities. He knew what He was about, knew what mattered and what didn't, and therefore concentrated His energies and time on the things conducive to accomplishing His purposes. Notice that everything Jesus came to be and to do involves us. His purpose was to give, to rectify, to purify.

And that's exactly how He spent His hours. He came to clear out obstacles and to die, but only to enable us to receive God's good for us. His purpose was not just to save us, but to make us pure and holy. Salvation is only a means to an end and not a purpose in and of itself. True, God can't do much with you while you're spiritually dead—any more than you can teach a child to talk or play until he's been born—but being born is only the beginning, not the goal.

So what do Jesus' purposes in life tell us about our own purposes in life? First, that we are to be abundantly alive *through Him;* He, in other words, is to be our lord. Second, we are to be enlightened so that we might know God. And third, we are to be pure and holy. These are the purposes that were important enough for God to send His Son on the climactic mission of all time.

Paul was also clear about his purpose. His work as an apostle was to ensure that Christ be formed in us, that we be complete in Christ, and that we walk in a manner worthy of God. "The goal of our instruction is love from a pure heart and a good conscience and a sincere faith" (1 Tim. 1:5).

If any one term summarizes Paul's purposes, it is Christian maturity, both for himself and for those to whom he ministered. He even says as much: God gave apostles, prophets, evangelists, pastors, and teachers "for the equipping of the saints for the work of service, to the building up of the body of Christ; until we all attain to the unity of the faith, and of the knowledge of the Son of God, to a mature man, to the measure of the stature which belongs to the fulness of Christ. As a result, . . . we are to grow up in all aspects into Him, who is the head, even Christ" (Eph. 4:11–15; see also 2 Cor. 12:19).

WHY GOD CREATED US

We've looked at Jesus' purposes and Paul's purposes. Now let's look at what the Bible says about our purposes.

There are a number of verses that state flatly why God created us. One is Revelation 4:11 (KJV): "O Lord, . . . thou hast created all things, and for thy pleasure they are and were created." Another is Isaiah 43:7 (KJV): "I have created him for my glory." God created us for His pleasure and for His glory. Those can sound like platitudes, so let's sharpen them.

God is love, so it is His nature to give; His greatest pleasure is having someone accept His gift of love and pass it on. This is why the fruit (singular) of the Spirit is love; if you have accepted His love and Spirit, your natural fruit is to exude to others the love that God is beaming into you.[1] We please God by "bearing fruit in every good work" (Col. 1:10).

We glorify Him the same way: "By this is My Father glorified, that you bear much fruit" (John 15:8). The fruit is love. The fruit is good works. Same thing. Love expresses itself in good works. God's purpose in creating us was that we please and glorify Him, and we do so when we bear His fruit of love and good works.

Love gets a lot of good press but good works gets a lot of

bad press because we evangelicals are conditioned to bristle when we hear the term *good works*. It is freighted with connotations of working one's way to heaven. But we're not talking about salvation here. Paul says that works without faith are dead and James says faith without works is dead. Neither is any good without the other.[2]

Perhaps not surprisingly, bearing fruit is also the purpose of our being believers. Jesus said, "I chose you, and appointed you, that you should go and bear fruit, and that your fruit should remain" (John 15:16).[3] Paul says the same: we died to law and have been joined to Christ "that we might bear fruit for God" (Rom. 7:4).[4]

GROWING UP

That is the doing part of our purpose in life. But what are we to be? As we've seen, we are to be holy and pure and righteous. But perhaps the one verse that best sums up all these ideas is Romans 8:29: "Whom He foreknew, He also predestined to become conformed to the image of His Son, that He might be the first-born among many brethren." All the various threads are fused together here. Our purpose in life is, simply, to become just like Jesus. Nothing less. That is why Paul's purpose was Christian maturity—with Jesus as the standard of maturity. No standard could be higher, but none lower would be worthy. We may settle for less, but God does not.

As our Creator, He knows what He created us to be, and He spelled it out right at the beginning: "Let Us make man in Our image, according to Our likeness" (Gen. 1:26). That primeval purpose has never changed, despite the diversion of our sin. The difference is that, whereas Adam was simply *made* in the image of God—period—we must now *become* conformed to the image of Christ. We must shed what Adam added as we become restored to the state he abandoned.

This "conforming" is not our own doing but God's doing. It is the goal of a gradual, lifelong process of becoming, growing, and maturing: putting off the old and putting on the new, as Paul expressed it. And one never attains complete conformity to Christ's image on this earth. But Jesus Himself does assure us that the maturing process will not be in vain: "A pupil is not above his teacher; but everyone, after he has been fully trained [perfected—Greek], will be like his teacher" (Luke 6:40; see also 1 John 3:2). In the meantime, "the one who says he abides in Him ought himself to walk in the same manner as He walked" (1 John 2:6).

Some Christians are born again but never grow. Others grow a little, figure that's plenty, then quit. But as Bob Dylan says, "He not busy being born is busy dying."* God means for us to grow up into Christ, and to the extent that we are not moving in that direction, we are not fulfilling our purpose in life.[5]

WHOEVER, HOWEVER, WHENEVER

Almost all of the various biblical expressions of the purpose of life are comprehended in the idea of becoming conformed to the image of Jesus. That is our purpose but is not something we can consciously *do* in a given situation. So the practical bottom line, the nugget to carry around in your pocket and apply in setting your priorities in each situation, is this: The purpose of life is to bear God's fruit of love and good works, that is, to give His love away to whoever needs it, however they need it, whenever they need it.

Does it matter whether we live out that purpose of life? In one sense, no, it doesn't. I mean, we don't have to; there's no one forcing us to. And most people don't. We can live our entire lives with no idea what the purpose is—or know it but ignore it—and the caliber of our lives will be no better or worse than that of the majority of the population.

But God does not use that standard of comparison. It may not matter to *me* whether I fulfill the purpose of life, but it certainly matters to the One who created me with that purpose

*From "It's Alright, Ma (I'm Only Bleeding)" by Bob Dylan. © 1965 Warner Bros. Inc. All rights reserved. Used by permission.

in mind. If I do not become more Christlike and loving, I'll still be a nice guy. You'll still like me. But—quite apart from any eternal consequences—I will have wasted my life.

By insisting, however, that my purpose in life is to be loving, I will make more loving decisions. I will have my priorities straight because they will be oriented toward that purpose like a compass needle. I will be less inclined to sulk when I don't get my way in a committee decision. If I don't like what the leaders at my church are doing, remembering the purpose will make me less likely to indulge in vicious gossip and destructive complaining. I'll be less likely to consider it my calling to lead a rebellion.[6]

God's primary purpose for us is that we *be*, specifically that we be loving and like Christ. The two are inseparable. To be genuinely one is to be genuinely the other.[7] I may claim a personal purpose more specific, but it will be valid only to the extent that it is an application of God's overall purpose.

It's also my own choice. God's purpose is general, not specific.[8] His purpose for me is identical to His purpose for you and for anyone else: to become conformed to the image of His Son and to love our neighbors. If we're *not* doing that, nothing else we do matters. If we *are* doing that, we are living a meaningful life.

NOTES

1. Galatians 5:22; 1 John 4:7–12.

2. See James 2:14–26. We certainly do not earn our salvation or score points with God for our fruit and good works: we are indeed saved by grace through faith. But Paul says in one breath that while we are not saved "as a *result* of works," we are "created in Christ Jesus *for* good works" (Eph. 2:8–10). They are the normal expression of faith and love. If the good works are missing, the faith and love are usually marginal. Something is plugging things up.

The problem is thinking of good works as something that we produce from our own carnal energy. But Jesus says "let your light shine before men *in such a way* that they may see your good works, and glorify your Father who is in heaven." (Matthew 5:16. See also 1 Peter 4:10–11 and 1 Corinthians 10:31.) Our good works should result in praise not to us, but to God— because they are not our fruit. They're His.

3. Here is Jesus' complete sentence: "I chose you, and appointed you, that you should go and bear fruit, and that your fruit should remain, that whatever you ask of the Father in My name, He may give to you" (John 15:16). Although our asking and His giving are the final point of His sentence, they are not the logical climax of His thought here. The point is bearing fruit; the asking and giving are to supply the nutrients needed to produce the fruit, not further purposes in themselves. Verse 2 reinforces the idea that the fruit is the purpose: "Every branch in Me that does not bear fruit, He takes away; and every branch that bears fruit, He prunes it, that it may bear more fruit."

4. In the next verse he contrasts this with bearing fruit for death.

5. The first thing to realize about Christian maturity is that God is the one producing the growth: Paul "planted, Apollos watered, but God was causing the growth" (1 Corinthians 3:6. See also Colossians 2:19 and Philippians 2:13.)

Second, God means business. What He is after is not improvement, but transformation (Rom. 12:1–2). With Jesus Himself as the standard, we have an impossibly long way to go, but God is in it for the long haul. We can bail out any time, but to the extent that we allow Him to, God is going to keep working in us *however He must* until He has conformed us to the image of Jesus. As C. S. Lewis says, "The goal towards which He is beginning to guide you is absolute perfection; and no power in the whole universe, except you yourself, can prevent Him from taking you to that goal. That is what you are in for" (*Mere Christianity*, 172). Paul says, "I am confident of this very thing, that He who began a good work in you will perfect it until the day of Christ Jesus" (Phil. 1:6; see also 2:13).

Third, growth comes through experiences, particularly difficult ones. This is why God does not normally bail us out of tough situations. Doing so would defeat His purpose in our lives. Rather, we should "consider it all joy, my brethren, when you encounter various trials, knowing that the testing of your faith produces endurance. And let endurance have its perfect result, that you may be perfect [that is, mature] and complete, lacking in nothing" (James 1:2–4; see also Romans 5:3–5 and 1 Peter 1:6–7; 5:10). James hastens to add that God is not sending the trials (v. 13). He doesn't have to. People being what we are, we'll produce quite enough trials naturally enough without their being divinely stirred up. God need only pick up on the trials as they come along and do His work in what we are.

The fourth thing to keep in mind about Christian growth is that God's Word is indispensable to the process. "As newborn babes, desire the pure milk of the word, that ye may *grow by it*" (1 Peter 2:2 KJV). Everybody changes over time, but the kind of spiritual growth God is after does not come apart from the Word. You'll only veer off cockeyed. John says we become strong to overcome Satan as the Word of God abides in us (1 John 2:14).

Fifth, Christian maturity does not nudge us off the deep end in any one direction, but results in a sober, conscientious balance. In a remarkable passage, 2 Peter 1:5-10, Peter urges us to diligently supplement one Christian virtue with another—and each of the seven he lists serves to correct tempting imbalances and excesses in the preceding one. The net result of all these qualities is a balanced character.

Sixth, as we mature we develop a godly wisdom—a wisdom from God, not our own (James 1:5)—to make mature judgments and decisions from loving motives. The mature, "because of practice have their senses trained to discern good and evil" (Heb. 5:14).

Finally, growth is vital not only for its own sake, but also because of the only alternative: mental, spiritual, and creative atrophy. Erich Fromm writes that "the amount of destructiveness to be found in individuals is proportionate to the amount to which expansiveness of life is curtailed. . . . Life has an inner dynamism of its own; . . . if this tendency is thwarted the energy directed toward life undergoes a process of decomposition and changes into energies directed toward destruction. . . . *Destructiveness is the outcome of unlived life*" (*Escape From Freedom*, 183–84).

6. This, I believe, is why Jesus consistently opposed the Zealots and why Paul and Peter say to obey the government. Their point is not that government is divine or satanic, but that we are believers whose purpose is to love—and rebellion is antithetical to that. Some rebellions may indeed correct certain wrongs, but they usually replace them with other wrongs and embitter lots of people in the process.

7. This pairing of loving and becoming more like Jesus (which is to say, Christian maturity) is reflected in Fromm's statement that "the ability to love as an act of giving depends on the character development of the person" (*Art of Loving*, 21).

8. I find nothing in the Bible to suggest that God wants me in one career or another, this ministry or that, living here or there. Those are all up to me as long as I make those decisions in conformity to God's general purpose for people. See chapter 17 for more about God's will.

13.

BEYOND THE PLATITUDES

In the last chapter we saw that our purposes in life are to become like Jesus and to bear his fruit of love. Unfortunately, we've all heard platitudes about love for so long that the idea has become flabby and toothless: "Oh, that again." So we need to look at love beyond the platitudes.

Jesus had little use for pleasant, passive benevolence toward nice people. He was after a get-your-hands-dirty involvement. To Him, love meant practical and persistent goodwill toward all, caring for others, and seeking their good.[1] In other words, the expression of being loving is doing loving things. "Let us not love in word, neither in tongue, but in deed and in truth" (1 John 3:18 KJV). As Erich Fromm says, *"Love is the active concern for the life and the growth of that which we love. . . . One loves that for which one labors, and one labors for that which one loves"* (*Art of Loving*, 22–23; italics his). Love, we might say, is measured in minutes and hours.

Love is like money: it doesn't do anybody any good until you pass it along. Indeed, love is not love *until* you pass it along, any more than your thighs are a lap until you sit down. But passing on God's love is not something that we can do legalistically or grudgingly. We are the salt of the earth, and salt does its job just by being its genuine self and giving itself away.

Paul's greatest statement on love is 1 Corinthians 13, the Love Chapter. There he says over and over, in effect, "Get your priorities straight! If I have all sorts of marvelous spiritual gifts and do all sorts of fine religious acts *but do not have love*, it profits me nothing and I am nothing. I can sell all my furniture, witness door-to-door every Saturday, lead three Bible studies a week, and spend an hour a day in prayer—I can do all that with love or without love, but it's the love and not the activity itself that counts."

Paul suggests something striking in his chapter on love: that the opposite of love is not hate, but pride. Love, he says, "is not jealous; love does not brag and is not arrogant, does not act unbecomingly; it does not seek its own, is not provoked, does not take into account a wrong suffered" (1 Cor. 13:4–5). Besides spelling out the things love is not, Paul says two things that love is: patient and kind. Patience implies a hopeful contentment with the present rather than an agitated, proud indignation that I don't yet have what I think I deserve. Kindness requires that I give of myself rather than expect something of others.

Everything pride is, love is not. Pride says, "I am first priority. I get mine to the exclusion of everybody else." But Jesus calls on us to love our neighbor *as* we love ourselves. With the same degree of attention. No more, no less.

It's a curious fact that the Bible never calls on us to love our neighbor *more* than we love ourselves. Such would not be a genuine love, but a neurotic excess and a veritable prescription for burnout, guilt, and a resentful family.[2] Loving your neighbor as you love yourself, though, is the very essence of balance, objectivity, moderation, humility—and the very antithesis of pride.

It is no coincidence that the one thing God hates above all else is pride, while the greatest commandment is to love.[3] "*Selfishness and self-love, far from being identical, are actually opposites,*" says Fromm. "The selfish person does not love himself too much but too little. . . . Selfish persons are incapable of loving others, but they are not capable of loving themselves either."[4]

NICE GUYS

The kind of love the Bible talks about is not the same as its cultural facsimile: niceness. Americans tend to place a surprisingly high priority on being nice. But niceness can easily be perverted. I am often too nice to want to embarrass someone by sharing Christ with them or by asking them to stop using my Lord's name in vain.

Psychologist Stanley Milgram conducted a now-classic experiment in the sixties in which he found that the majority of people would be very nice for an experimenter while electrocuting an innocent stranger at the experimenter's request. Psychologist Philip Zimbardo writes that one of the most significant discoveries of modern psychology is that a bare minimum of social pressure is sufficient to get people to do most anything: just having an authority figure touch a person's shoulder and say, "Do me a favor," is enough to get the person to eat grasshoppers, lie, act aggressively, and do all sorts of things the person wouldn't normally do. Why do people do it? Because we want to be nice guys, team players.[5]

Jesus never asks us to be nice in that sense. He wasn't a nice guy. He repeatedly embarrassed His hosts, when they had Him over for lunch, by lashing out at their Pharisaism or lecturing them on their pride. No sooner had He dismounted His donkey after the Triumphal Entry into Jerusalem—the peak of His popularity—than He alienated just about everyone by kicking the sellers and moneychangers out of the temple. He chose a moment when crowds were flocking to Him to stab at their superficiality. When a man asked Him to tell his brother to share the inheritance, Jesus said, "Man, who appointed Me a judge or arbiter over you?" and proceeded to lecture him and everyone around about greed. He embarrassed the man with the withered hand by having him stand up in front of the whole synagogue audience. When the Canaanite woman asked Him to exorcise the demon from her daughter, He parried, "I was sent only to . . . Israel. . . . It is not good to take the children's bread and throw it to the dogs." Son of God that He was, Jesus was not a nice guy.[6]

Neither was Paul. When he saw Peter's hypocrisy in refusing to eat with Gentiles, Paul told him off publicly. In his letter to the Galatians, he scoffs at the reputation of other apostles.[7]

Love is not the same as niceness, nor does it mean being wishy-washy. When Jesus preached, He scorched out the first ten rows. He was forever blistering the scribes and Pharisees. When a magician tried to turn the proconsul away from listening to Paul, the apostle blasted him: "You who are full of all deceit and fraud, you son of the devil, you enemy of all righteousness, will you not cease to make crooked the straight ways of the Lord?" (Acts 13:8–10).

In each of these cases, Jesus and Paul had very good reasons for treating the people involved the way they did. The context of each incident makes it clear that they wanted to defend the integrity of the gospel or drive home an important point, whether to the person addressed or to others in the audience. Though they were not being nice, their ultimate purpose in each case derived from a motive of love.

Since loving is our purpose in life, if we are not loving one another—no matter what else we might be accomplishing—we are worthless to God. I know that sounds harsh, but the Bible says it so often that we mustn't ignore it. Jesus is the vine of whom we are the branches, and "every branch in Me that does not bear fruit, [God] takes away. . . . If anyone does not abide in Me, he is thrown away as a branch, and dries up" (John 15:2, 6). "Every tree that does not bear good fruit is cut down and thrown into the fire."[8] Ground that yields thorns and thistles instead of vegetation "is worthless and close to being cursed, and it ends up being burned" (Heb. 6:7–8). John says, "He who does not love abides in death" (1 John 3:14), and Paul says, "If I . . . do not have love, I am nothing" (1 Cor. 13:2).

There is no assurance that people will welcome your love. They will often throw it back in your face. There is no assurance that, even with the most loving of intentions, you will be able to make a certain situation turn out a certain way. No one has to cooperate with your loving influence. People's interests are often so rigidly at odds that you may well be unable to convince both parties in a dispute that you are equally loving to each.

There is, in short, no assurance that your loving plans will succeed—only that love itself never fails.[9] It never fails in that loving invariably accomplishes God's will for you and satisfies His demands. Whatever the outcome of a given situation, if your role in it was genuinely and conscientiously loving, you did your job.

NOTES

1. Archibald M. Hunter, *A Pattern for Life*, 60.

2. Jesus came to minister to people, but always left plenty of time for Himself. Mark records that He was forever slipping off to the hills to be alone. Philippians 2:3 may, at first glance, seem to tell us to love our neighbor more than ourselves. But verse 4 clarifies the point: "Do not *merely* look out for your own personal interests, but *also* for the interests of others."

3. Proverbs 6:16–17; 8:13; 16:5; and others.

4. *Art of Loving*, 51, italics his. See also *Escape From Freedom*, 115.

5. "Mind Control: Political Fiction and Psychological Reality," *On Nineteen Eighty Four*, 207. For information about Milgram's fascinating experiment, see his book *Obedience to Authority: An Experimental View*.

6. Luke 11:37–54; 14:1–14; 19:35–46; 14:25–27; 12:13–15; 6:6–11; Matt. 15:22–26.

7. Galatians 2.

8. Matthew 7:19. In context this applies to false prophets, but fruit is the proof of each of us: "every tree."

9. 1 Corinthians 13:8. Let me warn against one misapplication of the Golden Rule. Boykin's Rule: Never surprise anyone with a favor. It is fine to do people favors, but never do one that they didn't ask for and don't know you're doing. Chances are your efforts will (1) be unwelcome, (2) foul things up, (3) irritate or offend the beneficiary, or (4) all of the above. I can cite no Scripture to support that. It's just a lesson of life I learn over and over. Nothing will sour one's faith in the Golden Rule as surely as getting burned by people who resent your well-intentioned surprise favor.

14. YOU DON'T HAVE TO

One of the most common reasons people give for what they do is that they have to. Why did I go to that meeting this morning? I had to. Why did the president send in the Marines? He had to. Why did your sister stay with her abusive husband so long? She had to.

The point of this chapter, though, is to show that, with a few kinds of exceptions, we do not in fact ever have to do anything. That idea can sound pretty ridiculous; we all do things all the time that we feel we have to do. But saying I did what I did because I had to is a non-reason that, though offered in all sincerity, fronts for the genuine reason. Until we cut through the assumption that people have to do things, we can never arrive at anything more than a shallow understanding of how people operate.

As an absolute principle, we always have choices; we do not have to do anything that we do not consent—however grudgingly—to go along with. No one can force you to do something if you decide to stick to a priority higher than the one their pressure exploits.

No doubt we can all think of extreme situations in which, for all practical purposes, we have to do a certain thing. But the fact remains that people sometimes *don't* do what they apparently have to do, even in the most extreme situations.

A young Cuban named Armando Valladares demonstrated the principle graphically under the most extreme kinds of circumstances. He was arrested as an enemy of the Cuban revolution after disobeying the law by praying in a church on Christmas Day 1960. In prison for twenty-two years, he was beaten daily, starved, and denied medical treatment for a fractured ankle and for festering rat bites. With ingenious cruelty his jailors tried to force him to deny his Christian faith, embrace communism, and wear the blue uniform of the "rehabilitated" prisoners.

He steadfastly refused, and began writing poetry to express both his pain and his hope. Using Mercurochrome as ink and a sliver of wood as a pen, he wrote on a blank prescription form: "For months I have been living on a concrete slab 2-½-feet wide by 6-feet long . . . but the narrower my physical space, the broader my spiritual horizons. The greater the repression and torture, the firmer and more resistant my internal framework. My situation is difficult, but I feel and am a free man."[1]

Valladares' experience, though extraordinary, is hardly unique. Comparable stories abound. After A.D. 70, when the Romans were wiping out Palestine, 967 Jewish Zealots made their last stand on the plateau fortress of Masada. For over two years they fought off their Roman attackers, until at last they realized that the next day the Romans would finally break through and overrun them. No hope remained. On that last night, their leader, El'azar, assembled the group: "It is evident that daybreak will end our resistance, but we are free to choose an honorable death with our loved ones. . . . Outrage, slavery, and the sight of our wives led away to shame with our children—these are not evils to which man is subject by the laws of nature: men undergo them through their own cowardice if they have a chance to forestall them by death and will not take it. . . . Let us die unenslaved by our enemies, and leave this world as free men in company with our wives and children."[2]

They therefore decided to take their own lives rather than let the Romans take them. Today every soldier of the Israeli army takes his or her vows atop Masada, symbol of the principle that in the most desperate of circumstances we are still free to make a choice.

Likewise, civil rights marchers in the United States, Gandhi's followers in India, and blacks in South Africa held political freedom as a priority even higher than they did avoidance of pain, so they took their stands and took their blows. Many were beaten senseless; some killed. But they refused to be forced to accept situations they considered unjust.

Philip Habib, who as the United States' special envoy to the Middle East in the early eighties mediated some of the most bitter, violent disputes imaginable (between Arabs and Israelis), negotiated day after day with people who were under enormous pressure from their enemies. He observes that "you can't force somebody to make a decision if he is willing to die in order not to make it."[3]

That does not, of course, mean that refusing to do what one apparently has to do is necessarily a good idea. When the volcano Mount St. Helens in Washington was about to erupt in 1980, people in the vicinity had to leave their homes lest they be killed by the imminent blast. One resident, named Harry Truman, stubbornly refused to leave his lodge at the foot of the volcano. When the sheriff's deputies came to order him to evacuate, he told them, in effect, "I don't have to leave if I don't want to." He didn't, and within days the volcano had buried him and his lodge under tons of ash and debris. The merits of his fatal decision are beside the point that he in fact did *not* have to do what everyone (with more common sense) thought they had to do.

In exercising choices in extreme situations, there is a fine line between heroic courage and folly—and maybe no line at all. Fools and heroes are distinguished by the wisdom of their actions and by the outcome—which may be entirely beyond their control. But whatever the merits or outcome of their decisions, heroes and fools both operate from the same value-neutral principle that you don't have to do anything you do not consent to go along with.

The options we might like to have in any situation, like walking away from it, may not be among the options open to us; but that doesn't mean we have no choices. The options may be few, all of them may be distasteful, and the consequences of doing anything other than what we apparently have to do may be unacceptable. Nonetheless, the options are real. No matter how dire the circumstance, how obvious the choice, how despicable or unthinkable the alternatives, or how unpleasant the consequences, we are free to choose a different option.

IT CUTS BOTH WAYS

Enough on extreme situations. The same principle applies in everyday life. You do not have to keep your same phone number if someone is pestering you by phone, stay in your present job, go to church, or show up to receive your Nobel Prize. You don't have to pay your taxes, take care of your children, or get out of bed in the morning. Perhaps you are *supposed* to do some of those things or you *should* do them, but that is another question. In an absolute sense you are not *forced* to. You and you alone have control of what your hands do, where your feet go, and what your mouth says.

In spite of obligations, expectations, traditions, or whatever you think forces you to do something, the principle that you do not have to do anything is absolute: you don't have to believe in God, obey the law, or be faithful to your spouse.[4] But it cuts both ways: neither do you as a Christian have to laugh politely at dirty jokes, assure someone that you're praying for them when you're not, bow to social pressure to drink at a party, or sit through a movie that turns out to be indecent. When someone insults you, you don't have to strike back. When someone cheats or abuses you, you don't have to get even.

You don't have to defend your "rights" (which may only be your pride), or squeeze out phony smiles for someone whom you can't stand (instead of talking out the problem). You don't have to spoil your children by giving in to their every whim and buying them everything they want or that you imagine they need. You don't have to deny your Lord at gunpoint or in polite company.

Do you consider it your God-appointed duty to help fellow Christians see the error of their ways by stirring up the gossip mill? Or carry out God's judgment on some miscreant of whom you self-righteously disapprove?[5] Or spread your negative opinion about the preacher? You don't have to. Nor do you have to work the whole family into a huff on Sunday morning insisting that everyone be spotless, or work yourself into a frazzle cleaning up the house for company.

Saying you don't have to can sound heartless or produce guilt feelings in some situations. But realizing the same principle can also be one of the most liberating experiences of your life. It can shake you out of a mindset whereby you let other people and your circumstances run your life. You don't have to give time to everyone who demands it—or who merely seems to need it—or live up to your parents', parishioners', or peers' expectations. You don't have to keep doing things the same old way. You don't have to get a pie baked in time for tonight's guests.

Some people feel that they must protect and perpetuate some lie they told or sin they committed (or that someone else committed against them) years ago. They've nursed it along for years and watched it fester into an enormous, foul master almost with a life of its own. They become so accustomed to living with it that, though it makes them miserable, they would rather keep hauling it around than deal with it once and for all and put it behind them. Psychologists coach people through such problems all the time, and their message over and over is *You don't have to live with that!*[6]

We often get lulled into attributing our own or other people's behavior to upbringing: "Oh, well, what do you expect of someone from a broken home?" Our upbringing does indeed have a powerful influence on us all our lives, but we mustn't hide behind that forever. There comes a point at which the most mistreated child becomes responsible for his or her own adult behavior. No one has to perpetuate his or her childhood.

MEANS TO AN END

If it is true that we do not have to do anything, then why are there so many things we *think* we have to do? Simply this:

They are a means—often the only means we can think of—to accomplish some end that we value. For example, I may have to run in order to catch the bus—but since when do I have to catch that bus? I can wait for the next one or take a cab or hitchhike or walk or go back home and forget the whole thing. Running is a means to one end, catching that bus is a means to another, reaching my destination is a means to another, and so on. I have to run only if I *choose* all those ends. I may have to fulfill a contract, but only if I want the other party to think well of me, pay me, continue to do business with me, or refrain from suing me. Fulfilling the contract may be my only means of accomplishing those ends, but I can always let some other consideration take precedence over them.

In each case, I have to do the means only if the ends are important enough to me. I am perfectly free to prefer other ends or to try other means.

What about duress? No one can force you to do anything; all they can do is give you incentives to encourage you to do it or threaten unpleasant consequences if you don't. Both kinds of leverage (in whatever form someone might apply them) work only if they appeal to and exploit a high priority of yours (such as staying alive, avoiding embarrassment, or saving money). To say that staying alive is a high priority to most people may not be terribly profound—but it does have the redeeming virtue of being true. Nonetheless, you are utterly free to insist on making something else a higher priority, in which case people's pressure loses its urgency. The variable is you.

Suppose, for example, someone pulls out a gun and demands that I reveal information that may put you in jeopardy. That person's only leverage over me is my own powerful desire to stay alive. But I may let something else— like protecting you—take priority. I therefore have choices. I can lie. I can distort the information enough to protect you. I can try talking my way out of the situation, try to escape, or fight. I can refuse to say a word. Or I can tell everything I know.[7] Even under duress I am not *forced* to do anything that I do not consent to go along with. If I feel that I have to do any one thing, it is only because I see that as the sole legitimate means to some end that I value. If my end is to save my own life, then I will probably feel that I have to talk. If, however, my higher end is to protect you, then I may feel I have to sacrifice myself as a means to that end.

As an absolute principle, though, I do not have to do either. I choose my end and the means to it according to what I want and what is most important to me.

By the same token, I may be so intent on the means that I don't even realize what end I am pursuing. If, for instance, I feel that I have to work overtime night after night, I may never question whether I am doing it to complete some project, impress people with my industriousness, keep from being bored, or avoid an unpleasant homelife. Working overtime may be a means to any or all such ends.

A FEW EXCEPTIONS

I said at the beginning of this chapter that there are a few kinds of exceptions to the principle that you don't have to.[8] One is actual physical constraint: being tied to a chair, grabbed by a stronger person, paralyzed—that sort of thing. If a band of kidnappers is physically dragging me out of my house, I have no choice about whether or not I will go with them because I have no control over my legs and arms. In such a case, I do have to go with them—but that's all I have to do.[9] Even in such an extreme situation, I still have other choices: Will I struggle or submit? Curse my situation or pray for wisdom and courage? Answer their questions or remain silent? Become bitter and hateful or adapt and adjust?

Those may be the only kinds of options open to me in an extreme situation, but they are genuine. Admiral James Stockdale, the highest ranking American naval prisoner of war in North Vietnam, was beaten and tortured many times in POW camps. He says that no matter what his captors did to him, even in the most dire situations, he always had a choice, even if it was nothing more than what his attitude would be.[10]

Jesus demonstrated the ultimate choice on the cross: although He could not move His body and had no freedom of action, He still *chose to forgive* those who put Him there. And ultimately, that's the kind of choice that matters, even in normal situations. No matter how desperate the situation or how certain the defeat, you can still make the kinds of choices that Christianity is really all about: forgiving and loving people.

A second kind of exception is that we do have to carry out bodily functions: we have to sleep, breathe, eliminate, and otherwise allow our body to do what it insists on doing. We can perhaps postpone any of them for a time, but the body will soon take over and do them in spite of us.

Notice, though, that while we have to allow the body to do its own functions, we do not have to do our part in servicing the body. Do you have to eat? Only if you want to ward off hunger pangs and stay alive. If, however, something is more important to you than staying alive, you don't have to eat. I know that sounds silly—everybody wants to stay alive—but I'm quite serious. In 1981 Irish Republican Army leader Bobby Sands went on a hunger strike to reinforce his demand that the British government grant political-prisoner status to himself and his IRA comrades in Ireland's Maze Prison. Sands refused food for weeks, eventually lapsed into a coma, and on the sixty-sixth day died. Another IRA member followed his example, then another and another, until after seven months ten IRA prisoners had starved themselves to death.

Regardless of what we might think of their cause, the point is simply that something was more important to them than staying alive. By their deaths they proved dramatically and conclusively that they did not have to do anything even as fundamental as eating, because they did not have to stay alive if they chose not to.

THAT TERRIFYING FREEDOM

A third exception to the principle that we don't have to, is that we do have to make choices—even when we might prefer not to. We don't have to choose this option or that one, but we do have to choose. Not only do we have the freedom to make choices, we are stuck with that freedom, whether we like it or not. Even when we relinquish our freedom, we do so freely.

The test of a person's character is what one does with what one perceives to be absolute freedom. Though we usually sense such freedom only in situations outside of normal (such as being alone in a strange city), the fact is that we *do* have absolute freedom to choose at all times and in all circumstances. Others may draw boundaries for us, but we decide for ourselves whether to keep within them. Those boundaries are like store windows: they keep us out (or in) only so long as we choose not to break them.

The vocation of human beings is to make decisions. That can be an oppressive responsibility, and some people will go to great lengths to evade or mitigate it.

It can be terrifying to realize the profound totality of human freedom. Erich Fromm wrote his classic book *Escape From Freedom* on the thesis that a person may be so frightened by the sense of isolation evoked by hard-core freedom that he will "seek a kind of security by such ties with the world as destroy his freedom and the integrity of his individual self," such as submitting to a fascist dictator, a repressive religious cult leader, or a sadistic spouse (*Escape From Freedom*, 22–23).

Freedom is dangerous and liable to abuse, which is why Christianity demands a sobering maturity. As Paul says, "All things are lawful for me, but not all things are profitable. All things are lawful for me, but I will not be mastered by anything" (1 Cor. 6:12). Whether as Christians or as atheists, we are free to do anything, but not everything is wise, moral, justified, legal, and so on.

Do you realize how perilously close Christianity is to anarchy? The only thing keeping Christianity from collapsing into the spaghetti of anarchy is the all-encompassing adequacy of the Holy Spirit within each believer. He is all there is, but He is all it takes.

It is no accident that Paul couples freedom to walking in the Spirit: "You were called to freedom, brethren; only do not turn your freedom into an opportunity for the flesh, but through love serve one another.... But I say, walk by the Spirit, and you will not carry out the desire of the flesh.... But if you are led by the Spirit, you are not under the Law" (Gal. 5:13, 16, 18).

If you come to Christianity expecting a set of rules and regulations to live your life by, you will be disappointed. Your local religious leaders may be only too happy to supply a set for you, but Jesus does not. Living the Christian life requires not religious laws, but the Holy Spirit, developing in us a godly maturity whereby we can cope with that terrifying freedom. Temptations are all around and we are free to give in to them, but we don't have to. "Our lower nature has no claim upon us; we are not obliged to live on that level" (Rom. 8:12 NEB).

What about our irresistible urges and impulses? Well, what's the difference between an "irresistible" urge and one that we simply *don't* resist? God, for His part, "will not allow you to be tempted beyond what you are able, but with the temptation will provide the way of escape also, that you may be able to endure it" (1 Cor. 10:13). In other words, God provides you with the inner resources to escape and endure—but it's up to you to apply those resources. He doesn't bail you out of the temptation (or trial or situation); he equips you inwardly to overcome it. "Therefore do not let sin reign in your mortal body that you should obey its lusts.... For sin shall not be master over you" (Rom. 6:12, 14).[11]

To say that we don't have to do things is not to deny the reality of the constraints under which we all operate, but rather to show that those constraints are binding only to the extent that we allow them to be. We often ask God or civil authorities to set us free; the most revolutionary thing we can realize, though, is that we *are* free.[12] We choose to do what we supposedly have to do. Our own wants and priorities—and not the thing itself—determine whether we "have to" do that something.[13]

Neither fate, predestination, events, politics, the economy, pressure, luck, vibrations from Saturn, nor even almighty God Himself forces us to do anything. We choose.

As long as we assume that we have to do certain things, we are in bondage to them. We will never let our creativity roam to try other, more satisfying, more godly, or more effective options. Only when we begin to see through such assumptions and imaginary constraints can we begin to realize our potential for freedom, creativity, success, and happiness.

But at the same time, we also begin to recognize our own responsibility for what we do. We can no longer blame our circumstances for our behavior. It's not that we should feel guilty for doing what we think we have to do, but simply that much of the pressure we feel is either imaginary, weak, or subject to our own will to overcome.

NOTES

1. *Reader's Digest*, "The Prisoner Castro Couldn't Break," by Sheldon Kelly, October 1983, 157–62). One of Valladares' fellow prisoners, Huber Matos, said after twenty years of comparable torture, "When a man has such a conviction, he develops tremendous inner strength. . . . No matter what they did to me, I could not give in. You can't break a human being who knows that he or she is right" (*National Review*, February 20, 1981, 184).

2. According to Josephus, *Jewish War*, reprinted in "Masada," a booklet published by the Israeli National Parks Authority, Government Printer, Jerusalem; inside back cover.

3. *The Stanford Magazine*, "Philip Habib: Whatever It Takes," interview by John Boykin, Spring 1984, 18.

4. Just as you do not have to do what people try to get you to do, neither do you have to yield to God. Your consent is the trigger in both cases. And just as there may be unpleasant consequences for withholding your consent from people, so are there eternal consequences for resisting God. But it's still your free choice.

5. See John 16:2–3.

6. After *Newsweek* magazine ran an article on sexual abuse of children, a woman wrote a letter to the editor to say, "I was abused when I was seven, and it has had a devastating effect on my life ever since. . . . Thank God victims of sexual abuse can now get [psychological] help. I don't have to live with my guilt anymore" (May 28, 1984, June Hayes, "Guilt and Innocence," 5).

7. Of course, any of those approaches may fail, simply because I cannot control how the person will react. I may get shot. Any given approach might be heroic or might be foolish. But the merits of the options or their likelihood of success are beside the point that options *are* open and that I don't have to do any one of them. I *choose* how to deal with the situation, and talking may be my choice. I may choose to gamble, and the gamble may or may not work.

8. There are also certain kinds of things that inhibit the exercise of our choice: unconscious habit, voluntary submission to someone else, lack of information or exposure (ignorance), lack of imagination, bad assumptions, surprise, reflex, fear, infancy, mental illness, medical incapacity, and perhaps a few others. Again, even in these situations, we do have choices, whether we think of them or not and whether we make them or not.

9. Strictly speaking, of course, going with the kidnappers is not something I *do*. The fact is not that I "go" with them, but that they carry me. The doing is theirs, not mine. If, however, instead of carrying me they shake a knife at me and order me to go, the going *is* then my doing, because my feet remain under my own control.

10. From a personal interview. Stockdale cites Victor Frankl who, in *Man's Search for Meaning*, said the same of his torture in a Nazi concentration camp. The one exception Stockdale says he might make is induced pain: someone threatening to break your bones unless you cooperate. But he stresses that this is the rare, rare exception. "Life isn't normally like that," he says. "Few people ever have the experience of someone breaking their bones."

11. That does not, of course, mean that if you just hang in there you won't ever sin. Sure you will. The point is simply that you don't have to give in to any particular temptation.

12. Jesus says truth sets us free (John 8:32). Why? Because it changes how we *think*. Politics, revolution, and the like don't set people free in the deepest sense. Embracing God's truth does.

13. This, of course, does not mean we should necessarily feel guilty about the things we formerly felt we had to go along with. That accomplishes nothing. The way to apply the idea is not to indulge an appetite for guilt but to own up to the choices we have been making, reconcile ourselves to the ones we are comfortable sticking with, and make the decisions necessary to break the cycle of constraints we are unwilling to remain bound to.

15. OF COURSE YOU CAN

The corollary to the principle that "you don't have to" is the principle that "you can." I'll begin this chapter by looking at "of course you can" from the direction of "why you don't."

Although nothing and no one can force you to do something you refuse to do, there are plenty of things that can inhibit or prevent you from doing what you want to do. The inhibition I want to concentrate on here is the one inside our own heads.

Any homemaker will tell you that you can't refreeze meat. But you most certainly can. Just pop it back in the freezer. You will ruin it if you do, but you can. Now, that sounds like trivial bickering over words, but actually it gets at a very important principle: I can do anything that requires only a decision on my part to do. My choice may be wise, noble, and sound, or it may be foolish, premature, and disastrous—but it's still my choice. I am perfectly free to make stupid decisions. I prove that by doing so, more often than I would like to admit.

At the opposite end of the spectrum, President Lyndon Johnson, when he found himself getting drawn deeper and deeper into the Vietnam war, said, "I feel like a hitchhiker beside a Texas highway during a hailstorm. I can't run, I can't hide, and I can't make it stop."[1] A hitchhiker may be in that position, but Johnson was not. Of course he could have stopped American involvement in Vietnam. From hindsight, pulling out might have been the wisest thing he could have done. He didn't, not because he couldn't, but because the likely political consequences of doing so were unacceptable to him. I'm not suggesting that he should or should not have, only that he *could* have. He chose not to.

So the principle is the same, whether we're talking about something as trivial as refreezing meat or as monumental as pulling out of Vietnam: So long as the decision is yours to make, you can do it. And the principle is true whether other people would make the same choice or not. One person says, "I can't let him walk all over me," while another says, "I can't do anything about it." One says, "I can't find the time to pray," while another says, "I can't make it without prayer."

Often, the problem is not that we are unable to do the thing, but rather that we are unable to reconcile doing that with doing something else that is more important to us. I say I can't join you for dinner Thursday night because I have other plans, but the fact is that my present plans are more important to me than is your dinner. I can't do both, so I prefer to stick to my original plans.[2]

Much of what we consider impossible is merely improbable. For instance, I may think it impossible that I would ever spend a night in Buckingham Palace, but as soon as I ask why, I realize that the queen is never likely to invite me and that the guards there are not likely to let me stay uninvited. But if staying in Buckingham Palace were really that important to me—if I made it first priority—I would set about coming up with some way of doing it. I may still fail because I lack other people's cooperation, but if I consider it impossible from the outset, I will never tackle the goal at all. As Henry Ford said, "Those who believe they can do something and those who think they cannot, are both right." All things are impossible to him who does not believe.

A FEW GOOD ODDBALLS

The principle that you can is easy to ridicule because there are so many things you *can* do that nobody is fool enough to actually do. But the principle is well worth locking in on, because Jesus calls on us over and over to do precisely the unthinkable: invite the poor to dinner rather than friends (lest they return the invitation); stop whatever you're doing and suddenly leave friends, family, and co-workers behind to follow Him; give to whomever wants to borrow from you; get rid of anything that makes you stumble, no matter how precious it is to you; do not strike back at people for the nasty things they do to you; pray for those who persecute you; love your enemies. If someone wants to sue you for your shirt, give him your coat too. Jesus not only ridicules worry, he forbids it.

Ridiculous stuff. But Jesus doesn't blink in demanding such things. The Sermon on the Mount is chilling when you realize that Jesus means exactly what He says. "Nowhere is there to be found [in the Sermon on the Mount], as there is in Paul, reflection upon the inability of men to fulfill the will of God, but rather the astonishing fact that Jesus expected from his disciples that they would do what he commanded. He addresses himself throughout [the sermon] to the will of men" (Joachim Jeremias, *The Sermon on the Mount*, 8).

The things Jesus demands are entirely foolhardy—until you begin to share His view of things. Come to see money not as a passport to luxury but as a dangerous encumbrance, and you will not find it so ridiculous to give to whomever wants to borrow. Realize that your purpose in life is to give His love away, and you will find it easier to refrain from striking back at people who hurt you.

We sometimes hear people snort at these feeble little principles of Christianity—love your neighbor, pray for your enemies, consider the lilies—and mutter, "Yeah, but you can't run society that way." Probably not. But Jesus had no interest in running society. His aim was and is to run people—a few here and there. We're to be the salt of the earth—not the meat and potatoes. Jesus is looking for a few good oddballs, people willing to do what to the world makes no sense, because it's important to them.

Choosing the unthinkable option takes courage, a Spirit-inspired imagination, and a recognition that you *can* choose the narrow gate instead of the wide road everyone else is on.

SETTLING FOR MEDIOCRITY

Paul says, "I can do all things through Him who strengthens me" (Phil. 4:13), and Jesus says, "Apart from Me you can do nothing" (John 15:5). We should always take these two statements together lest we fall into the I-can-do-nothing mentality that all too often passes for humility. Jesus was talking about His being the vine—*all* of the vine—of which we are the branches: apart from Him we can do precisely nothing *as branches*. But that doesn't mean that apart from Him no one can do anything, period. Ninety-five percent of the population does a hundred percent of their activity—good things, bad things, moral, immoral, you name it—apart from Him. But no one can do anything *as a branch* of Christ apart from Him. I may put all my dollars in the plate, spend hours in prayer, and memorize dozens of Scripture verses, but if I don't have His Spirit in me, I have not done anything as a branch. I can imitate Christianity, but I can't *live* it apart from Him.

Many Christians feel more comfortable with the idea that apart from Christ they can do nothing, than they do with the other side of that coin: that they can do all things through Him who strengthens them. "I can do nothing" lets me off the hook; "I can do all things" makes me wonder why I'm not doing anything. It's easier to piddle around wondering whether it's God's will that you rent this apartment or that one, than it is to face up to God's ultimate will for you: that you become conformed to the image of His Son.

He, in other words, is not settling for mediocrity in you. He has the highest imaginable plans for you. It's a tall order, entirely beyond our human capabilities. But He's already started reconstruction. "A pupil is not above his teacher; but everyone, after he has been fully trained [perfected—Greek], will be like his teacher" (Luke 6:40). We are not there yet, but the only limitation is the extent to which we are willing to yield. "Now we are children of God, and it has not appeared as yet what we shall be. We know that, when He appears, we shall be like Him, because we shall see Him just as He is" (1 John 3:2).

We can't imitate Jesus convincingly or for long, and in that sense we must recognize our failure and limitations. But if His Holy Spirit is in you, you have no business settling for mediocrity, insincerity, and failure. Because if you are indeed a branch, you are not limited to your own limitations. Failure does not have to be final, because there is a whole 'nother factor at work in you: the Holy Spirit. It's a quantum difference. You can't but He can. And if He is in you, the new you can.

NOTES

1. Stanley Karnow, *Vietnam: A History* (New York: The Viking Press, 1983), 396.

2. I may in fact want to dine with you more than I want to do what I had planned, but the very equilibrium of sticking with the plan may itself be what takes priority over dining with you. It is not necessarily *un*important to me to join you; it's just that something else is *more* important.

16.　　　　　COOPERATION

We saw last chapter that we can do anything we please that requires only a decision on our own part. We saw in a prior chapter that we don't have to do anything that we do not consent, however grudgingly, to go along with. Someone can raise the stakes so that non-cooperation becomes more and more unattractive to me, but in the final analysis, I, and I alone, control what words my mouth says and what actions my body takes.

This brings us to the doorstep of the principle that power or authority resides not in the powerful person, but in the people who obey. Whether we are talking about the power of a political leader, a union boss, an employer, a spouse, or an influential peer, the principle is the same. Power is a relationship in which other people cooperate with someone's expressed or assumed wishes. The powerful person can yell and connive and threaten all he wants, but if the followers merely withdraw their allegiance and obedience, the powerful person suddenly loses "his" power—because it was never his in the first place.

For example, the last Shah of Iran ruled his country with an iron fist for over two decades. Throughout the sixties and most of the seventies he was one of the most stable and powerful dictators in the Middle East. In 1978, though, his people revolted and finally chased him out of the country. His power evaporated. The Shah didn't change. Other people did. The measure of their support was the measure of his power.[1]

Power may be based on any number of factors, most commonly things like:

> personal charisma
> violence

election, appointment, or being hired
position (e.g., parent)
social standing (e.g., elder)

But none of these factors in itself bestows power. A person's power hangs on two criteria: (1) you must exploit it to get people to do what you want, and (2) they must cooperate. If either criterion is missing, there is no power. Between the command and the implementation is a human being who may choose to obey or disobey.

HOLDING SOCIETY TOGETHER

As long as this is so, any kind of organization is only a decision away from anarchy. The glue that holds society together at every level, therefore, is made of cooperation and consistency. When people cooperate, we call their cooperative enterprise a company, a system, the Mafia, a government, an army, whatever. Such verbal shorthands for their enterprise are convenient, but we make a silly mistake when we begin to attribute to their enterprise some impersonal, absolute, invincible, self-perpetuating character. Whatever the group—the Democratic party, IBM, "international communism," the Catholic church—it's nothing more nor less than people cooperating, and that cooperation consists of things individual people decide and do. Army ants.

Consistency is as important as cooperation for holding society together. By *consistency* I mean our tendency to hold to previous decisions and thereby act in predictable ways. Abiding by yesterday's decisions is one of the most powerful reasons behind today's decisions. If people cooperated yesterday, they are likely to do so again today. And if they didn't yesterday, they probably won't today either. We base many decisions on the consistency of the postal workers, the consistency of the farmers and grocers, the consistency of foreign governments abiding by treaties.

Sometimes people's cooperation and consistency work to

our advantage, sometimes to our disadvantage. It depends primarily on *whom* they are cooperating with! If you are in jail and want out, the guards can easily release you. It would take only two minutes of their time. And if by bribery or some other means you succeed in getting their cooperation, you can get out.[2]

But prison guards normally cooperate, not with their prisoners, but with the warden, who in turn is cooperating with the judge, who is cooperating with the governor and the legislators—all of whom are cooperating with the voters. No one in the chain is *forced* to cooperate, but we expect that each will anyway. And recognizing the fragility of that chain of cooperation, the people at each level have prepared certain unpleasant consequences for anyone who *doesn't* cooperate consistently.

Your success in any endeavor will often depend on the cooperation of others.[3] If you try to earn a living as an artist, for instance, your success will depend on whether people cooperate by buying your creations or tickets to your performances. If they do, you will succeed; if they don't, you will fail. If you want to get admitted to Harvard, elected to office, hired for a job, or accepted as a tenant, the determining factor will be the cooperation of the right people.[4]

No force—God or fate or your lucky star—can by-pass people's cooperation to "give you success" in any of these kinds of endeavors without depriving those people of their capacity to decide. To ask God to intervene in your circumstances by, say, getting you admitted to Harvard, is to ask Him to make the admissions officers' decisions for them and in spite of them.

Sometimes we should cooperate, other times we should not, and wisdom is what enables us to judge when either is appropriate. You probably should cooperate when the police officer signals for you to pull over, but your teenage son probably should not cooperate when his friends want him to help break into a car. Moses chose not to cooperate with Pharaoh. Jesus sometimes cooperated with His captors by answering their questions, other times He stood silent. The choice rests with us as to whether or not we will cooperate and do someone else's bidding.

JUST RAISING THE PRICE

"That's all fine in theory," people say to me. "But what about people who live in repressive countries *today?* Surely you don't think they are free to do as they please." Yes, they most certainly are. The same principle applies. The *consequences* of non-cooperation are far more unpleasant for those under a malevolent dictator, but those people are still entirely free to do as they choose. They, of course, quickly learn to be circumspect about *exercising* that freedom—they probably won't spit at the police or preach on the street corners—but they still *can* as long as they are willing to accept the likely consequences. Their choice.

Whether the act is smuggling Bibles into Bulgaria (with the consequence that you get arrested) or telling a client the truth (with the consequence that you lose a sale), the principle is the same: You make a decision and accept the consequences. If you are unwilling to risk arrest, don't smuggle Bibles into Bulgaria. If, however, your first priority is the kingdom of God, you just might be willing to risk arrest to get the Word of God into people's hands. People do that. It's illegal. The consequences are stiff. But as long as they are willing to risk those consequences, they are perfectly free to do it.

"Yes, but what about the risk of getting killed?" we ask. It may sound heartless to say, but that's no different. People take those risks, and some get killed. The freedom to choose is absolute. The apostle Paul was beaten, stoned, flogged, cussed out, and eventually executed for preaching the gospel. Did persecution stop him? Of course not. It might stop me, it might stop you, but it doesn't stop everyone. We each make our own choices. In fact, nothing galvanizes believers more than does persecution. That has nothing necessarily to do with the merits of their beliefs: people of any religion tend to strengthen their resolve in the face of persecution. I might not. I don't like pain. But there are countless examples of people who *have* risked and suffered pain and even death under repressive governments rather than renounce their beliefs.

Repressive governments do get overthrown—but only when enough people or the right people become willing to accept the consequences of challenging them. People in Poland formed the Solidarity trade union in 1980, went on strike, marched, protested, and made demands of the communist government. They proved that they were free to do it by doing it!

There were of course reactions: government soldiers cracked heads and the Polish prime minister banned Solidarity and declared martial law. Had the Polish soldiers cooperated with the Solidarity members rather than with the government leaders (as some nearly did for a time), Solidarity might have won. It's not unheard of: the turning point in the 1978 revolution against the Shah of Iran came when his soldiers stopped fighting the revolutionaries and joined them. In both countries the citizens made their choices, the government leaders made theirs, and the soldiers made theirs. Each was free to and each did.

There is no assurance of success, no assurance of cooperation from other people—only the absolute freedom of each human to make his or her own choices. You may decide to cooperate rather than risk arrest or death. That's fine: you have made your choice. Ninety-nine percent of the population may do the same thing, but the option is *always* open to decide the other way.

Some do. Mohandas Gandhi once wrote, "It is my certain conviction that no man loses his freedom except through his own weakness. Even the most despotic government cannot stand except for the consent of the governed which consent is often forcibly procured by the despot. Immediately the subject ceases to fear the despotic force, his power is gone" (*Gandhi: Selected Writings*, 280). The same point was made concisely in a sign on the casket of assassinated Philippine opposition leader Benigno Aquino in 1983: "There are no tyrants if there are no slaves."

WHAT IS YOUR TYRANT?

An oppressive government makes the most convenient example of the principles at hand, but that is probably not the kind of tyrant you face. What is your tyrant? The opinion of your friends? Your spouse, religious leader, professor, employer? Perhaps some imaginary standard that you legalistically think you must live up to? You don't have to. You choose to.

Whatever or whoever is "forcing" you to compromise your principles, conceal your faith, or singe your conscience numb is a master of your own making. If you are content with that master, fine: you have made your choice and will live with the consequences of it until you choose to break that relation. But if you are cooperating with some tyrant and are *not* content to continue, you are just as free to stop as you were to begin. "Tyrannies," says psychologist Stanley Milgram, "are perpetuated by diffident men who do not possess the courage to act out their beliefs" (*Obedience to Authority*, 10).

The consequences of making a break may be unpleasant, but if you are willing to risk them, you are free to do it. The purpose here is not to suggest what your choice *ought* to be in any given circumstance, only to insist that you almost invariably do have a choice, and should own it. You do not have to perpetuate yesterday's bad decisions.

We are, in other words, free to live by our convictions if we are *willing* to live by our convictions.[5] The greatest and ultimate inhibition is not external, but internal. God promises a way of escape from any temptation; one of the most effective ways of escape is the simple realization that you don't have to go along with that temptation.

Living by your convictions will cost you something every time you make a choice between Christ and a competing interest. It may cost you embarrassment, friends, sales, a job, in some extreme situations even your mobility or your life. Those are all heavy prices to pay, but that's what we're in for if we mean to follow Jesus. "Count the costs," He says. "Which comes first: a sale, a friend, embarrassment—or Me? With whom are you going to cooperate?"

If that frightens you to read, it frightens me to write, because I, probably like you, don't want to make such choices. And if I must make them, I don't want to admit what I'm choosing over what. But my reluctance and yours does not deflect the jab of Jesus' words: "Seek ye first the kingdom of God."

NOTES

1. His followers, of course, weren't the only ones who changed. The Shah held power as long as he did largely because he enjoyed the support of the United States.

2. Don't laugh; it's been done. Reuters reports that on October 21, 1985, all 149 inmates at the Central Jail in Honiart, the Solomon Islands, "strolled away . . . after guards opened the gates as a protest." The guards "complained that a recent compensation award to a prisoner who said that he had been beaten by guards made it impossible to control inmates effectively." So they just let them out. (*San Francisco Chronicle*, Oct. 22, 1985, "Angry Jailers Let Loose 149 Inmates.")

3. In that sense, politicians' and diplomats' efforts to devise nuclear strategy is essentially no different from parents' efforts to keep their teenagers under control. In both cases they are trying strategies calculated to insure the adversary's behavior—and in neither case do they have the slightest assurance that their strategy will have the desired effect, for the simple reason that people are unpredictable and uncontrollable if they don't consent to be controlled.

4. That is not to downplay the importance of ability and perseverance; simply to recognize that countless able and persevering people do not succeed in these kinds of endeavors because others did not cooperate with them.

5. We need never ask God for the "grace" to do so; He's given us that already. We're not waiting for Him to supply the grace; He's waiting for us to take the step.

17.   GOD'S WILL

A friend once told me she had just quit her job because she felt it was God's will to do so. She asked for prayer that He would now show her which other job He had prepared for her. Before long—and after a series of striking coincidences—she heard of a job that seemed ideal. The coincidences were just too remarkable to attribute to chance; this had to be God's leading, so she took the job, praising God for His providence.

By the time I next saw her several months later, she had decided it was God's will that she leave her new job. Besides, the work was boring and she and her boss did not get along. Would I again pray that God might lead her to the next job He had for her?

This went on several times. It wasn't just jobs, but activities and other aspects of her life. In time it became apparent that God was no more leading her in and out of things than He was washing her windows. She was just flaky. Sincere, but quite immature and utterly unreliable.

What she was doing, though, was just what any good evangelical is taught to do: interpret circumstances as God's doing and seek His will in deciding what to do about them. I've already argued that the first point, reading God's hand into circumstances, is a mistake because He normally doesn't operate that way. Here let's focus on the second, whether God normally tells us what to do (or what His will is) in and through our circumstances.

Trying to discover and do God's will is a prime preoccupation of countless believers. Along with habitually reading God's hand into circumstances, it is considered a prime indicator of spirituality. We pack out seminars and snatch up books that offer a biblical formula for discovering God's will. As we discussed in the chapter "Does God Control?" what we usually want to know is God's "individual" will—what He wants each of us individually to do in each situation. Is it God's will that I major in this subject or that? Does He want me to join this group or that one, take this trip or not?

The custom of seeking God's individual will, though, is one of the most frequently abused in Christendom. You've no doubt known some believers like my job-hopping friend who seem all too eager to pronounce their own ideas God's will. His will becomes a Rorschach pattern onto which we project our own inclinations. For example, women used to come up to gospel singer Andraé Crouch all the time and say that God had told them they were to be his wife. Crouch always marveled that God was telling so many women that—while neglecting to fill *him* in on the plan! When a famous TV preacher claimed in 1977 that Jesus had told him to raise $240 from each of his followers to fund some project, many Christians faithfully sent in their checks—but many more considered it a cynical ploy for money.

When someone with whom we sympathize claims that such and such is God's will, we tend to go along; but when someone we mistrust claims that *his* idea is God's will, we smell a rat.

While some believers leap to conclusions about God's will, most believers seem more accustomed to the opposite position—having not the slightest idea what God wants them to do in most situations. We practice reading the tea leaves of coincidences, impressions, and open doors to augur His well-hidden will. But it remains as hidden as ever.

As a result, many believers become paralyzed when faced with a decision because, try as they might, they simply haven't a clue what God's will is. Does He want me to do this or that? How can I decide if He's not telling? Do I not have enough faith, or am I just not reading the signs correctly?

HERESY?

I would suggest that the problem is neither insincerity nor faulty will-finding technique. The problem is a faulty assumption that God has an individual will to be found at all.

God is vitally interested in how you live out your Christian life minute by minute (since that's the only way you *can* live it), and He is therefore certainly interested in whom you marry, where you live, and which job you take. But those are not the kinds of things His will is all about. When the Bible talks about "God's will," it is usually not talking about details of our experience, but about sweeping, fundamental issues. For example, here are the things the New Testament says in so many words are God's will:

> that we be sanctified rather than sexually immoral (1 Thess. 4:1–7)
>
> that we be filled with the Spirit (Eph. 5:17–18)
>
> that we live in the Spirit (1 Peter 4:6)
>
> that we silence critics by doing right, such as submitting to human authorities and abstaining from fleshly lusts (1 Peter 2:11–17)
>
> that we rejoice always, pray without ceasing, and give thanks in everything (1 Thess. 5:16–18)
>
> that elders shepherd the flock voluntarily and eagerly, rather than under compulsion or for sordid gain (1 Peter 5:2)
>
> that all who believe in Jesus may have eternal life and be raised by Him on the last day (John 6:39–40)
>
> that Paul be an apostle (1 Cor. 1:1; and elsewhere)
>
> that the Macedonians give themselves to the Lord and to Paul (2 Cor. 8:5)
>
> that Jesus deliver us out of this present evil age (Gal. 1:4)
>
> that we be holy and blameless, adopted as sons of God through Jesus (Eph. 1:4–5)
>
> that we be the firstfruits among His creatures (James 1:18)

> that if we suffer (in persecution), it be for doing right
> rather than for wrong (1 Peter 3:17; 4:19)

At first it may seem heretical to suggest that God does not have an individual will for every detail of our lives,[1] but the suggestion is entirely consistent with two of the major principles of the New Testament: that God is far more interested in what we are than in what we do and that we are not under law but under grace.

Looking to God for ad hoc psychic direction in each situation is only a short step away from looking to Him for written rules and regulations for each situation. Both derive from a legalistic outlook, both seek to evade the responsibility of making mature decisions,[2] and both miss the point of how God relates to His people.

GUIDANCE

The idea of an individual will of God hinges on the idea of guidance, the assumption that God somehow communicates His individual will to us on an ad hoc basis. Accordingly, one of the more frequently heard prayers is "show us your will." But the only instance in Acts of anyone praying specifically for guidance occurs before Pentecost when Peter—who else?—had the great idea that somebody should take Judas' place. The believers put forward two candidates, Joseph and Matthias, and *then* prayed, "Show which of these two Thou hast chosen" (Acts 1:24 KJV). They then flipped a coin, Matthias won, and the Eleven welcomed their new colleague.

But there is no suggestion in the narrative that God gave them any input in their nominating process or that He took any part in their coin toss. While they by flipping a coin chose Matthias (who is never heard from again), God had chosen someone they had not yet heard of, Saul of Tarsus. The pursuit of ad hoc guidance thus got off to a bad start, and the Bible never records another instance of anyone asking for it again.

People of course *got* guidance now and then, but never in

response to asking for it. God, on His own initiative, occasionally gave an apostle specific instructions about what to do, but there is no record of any "ordinary" believer receiving direct guidance.[3]

Nor did even the apostles receive guidance on a regular basis. In the thirty years or so covered by the book of Acts, there are at most fifteen to twenty instances of direct, personal guidance—usually to Paul.[4] And in each apostolic instance, it was clearly a *miraculous* revelation: a vision, a voice, an angel. When anyone received guidance, it usually had to do with the spread of the gospel. Nowhere in the New Testament does anyone ever ask God to show them His individual will about what to do in a specific mundane situation. Nowhere does God do so by any of the kinds of means whereby we today expect Him to (such as inward impressions, peace, circumstances, open doors, and so on). Nowhere does anyone say they made such and such a decision because they *felt* it was God's will.[5]

But aren't there lots of verses that talk about God's individual will? Garry Friesen, chairman of the Bible Department at Multnomah School of the Bible, did an extensive study of God's will, which resulted in his excellent book, *Decision Making and the Will of God*. There he analyzes the various Scriptures usually cited to establish the idea of God's individual will and concludes, "A superficial reading of the passages does provide a foundation for the traditional view [of an individual will] that is scriptural. But closer scrutiny reveals that foundation to be inadequate. For in order to arrive at the conclusion of the traditional approach, it is necessary to water down the biblical examples and spice up the biblical teaching" (112). Those verses, Friesen shows, each apply to God's "moral" will, His general principles that apply equally to all believers.

Friesen observes that, though we may believe we should seek the one particular option God has for us in each choice, we all at some point abandon that approach to making decisions simply because, theory aside, it is utterly impossible to live by.

We must make too many decisions in any given hour to consult the tea leaves about each one.

This can be verified by a simple test: "During the past week, in what percentage of the decisions that you made did you have certainty of knowing God's individual will in advance? While you are computing, don't overlook such choices as which route you took to work, which pew you sat in at church, which shoe you put on first each morning, and which particular fruit you selected at the grocery store" (*Decision Making*, 120). At what level of triviality does God's individual will cease to apply? If it applies to the *n*th degree, then how can any believer possibly seek it in each minute decision and still function as a sane human being?

The reason we so regularly fail to find God's individual will for us is that there is no such will to be found. Sometimes we may take comfort in imagining that God has somehow told us which option to choose; other times we draw a blank. But in neither case is God trying to whisper in your ear. He doesn't normally work that way.

Friesen's "*major point* is this: God does not have an ideal, detailed life-plan uniquely designed for each believer that must be discovered in order to make correct decisions. The concept of an 'individual will of God' cannot be established by reason, experience, biblical example, or biblical teaching. . . . Not only is the individual will of God not found in Scripture, but the suggested process for finding it is absent as well" (*Decision Making*, 145–46; italics his).

MATURE, GODLY DECISIONS

If God does not have an ad hoc will for us individually, then what does the Bible mean when it talks about His will? It is referring to general principles for life, which apply to all believers equally and which are fully revealed in the Bible. God does not tell you as a Christian whom to marry; He just says not to marry unbelievers. He does not tell you which church to go to; He just says not to forsake assembling with other believers.[6]

The Holy Spirit is in the business of transforming you by renewing your mind[7]—which you are expected to use to make mature, godly decisions. He gives us a spirit, not of timidity, but of power, of love, and a sound mind; specifically, the mind of Christ.[8] God provides His Word as the food for us to grow on as we practice and bump our heads and train our senses to discern good and evil. He develops in us a godly wisdom if we let Him, a wisdom by its nature pure, peaceable, gentle, reasonable, full of mercy and good fruits, unwavering, and without hypocrisy.[9]

God, in short, equips us with all the inner resources we could need to make wise, mature, godly decisions. We waste those resources when we hold off making a decision until we see a "sign" or feel some psychic vibration. That's not faith; it's card reading.

One of our purposes in life is to become spiritually mature; asking God to relieve us of the need to make decisions by making things happen without us or to make our decisions for us is antithetical to growth. It is indeed a hallmark of spiritual immaturity.

God does not equip us inwardly for the purpose of making us better able to figure out His will. Rather, knowing His (moral) will is only a means to an end: you are to "be filled with the knowledge of His will ... *so that* you may walk in a manner worthy of the Lord, to please Him in all respects, bearing fruit in every good work and increasing in the knowledge of God" (Col. 1:9–10). The purpose of knowing God's will is to walk in a *manner* worthy of the Lord. That's general. It's pleasing Him in *all* respects, bearing fruit in *every* good work—whatever good work you might decide to do.

The key word is *whatever*. "Whatever your hand finds to do, verily, do it with all your might" (Eccl. 9:10). "Whatever you do in word or deed, do all in the name of the Lord Jesus. . . . Whatever you do, do your work heartily, as for the Lord rather than for men" (Col 3:17, 23; see also Titus 2:7–8). Over and over the Bible emphasizes that what counts with God is not what you do, but what you are, and how and why you do what you do. "As for the pure, his work is right"—whatever his work may be, since it proceeds from a pure heart (Prov. 21:8 KJV).

Does God want you to go preach in Africa? Possibly, yet He probably isn't that specific. But He certainly does want you to let your light shine wherever you are. And if you're not doing so now, what makes you think you will in Africa?

Was it God's will that any given believer in Corinth eat or not eat meat offered to idols? Neither. It wasn't a matter of God's will at all, but of individual conscience. "Whether, then, you eat or drink or whatever you do, do all to the glory of God" (1 Cor. 10:23–33).

CHEAP GLORY

Notice that there is a world of difference between "doing all to the glory of God" and the common but vacuous notion (discussed in chapter 4, "Does God Control?") that whatever happens—and therefore whatever anybody does—is ipso facto God's will and therefore accrues somehow to God's glory. The idea is that it is God's will that people do nasty things so that His glory will be highlighted by the contrast. So when a man rapes a woman, someone spreads false doctrine, a drunk driver slams into a school bus, or an unbeliever rejects God for the final time, we presumably should praise God that He's more glorious than anyone who would do such things. By such reasoning we portray God's glory as a meaningless black hole enhanced by anything and everything anybody does.

Jesus does not endorse that notion. He defines precisely how God can be glorified in our behavior: "By this is My Father glorified, that you bear much fruit [that is, love], and so prove to be My disciples" (John 15:8). "Let your light shine before men *in such a way* that they may see your good works, and glorify your Father" (Matt. 5:16). Peter says the same: "Keep your *behavior excellent* . . . so that . . . they may on account of your good deeds . . . glorify God" (1 Peter 2:12). God is not glorified by whatever anybody happens to do. Rather, believers are supposed to behave in ways and according to motives that *do* glorify God.

The bottom line is that we do God's will when we agree with Him, which is to say, when we value what He values. When we want what He wants, we will do what He wants because it will be what we want too. When what is important to Him is important to us, we will do it. Any other kind of obedience—whether to His will or to His law—is grace-age legalism.

God's will is indistinguishable from His purposes for us. His will, in a word, is that we fulfill our purposes in life: to bear Christ's fruit of love and to become conformed to His image, "that He might be the first-born among many brethren" (Rom. 8:29). This, I believe, is why Jesus says, "Whoever does the will of God, he is My brother" (Mark 3:35). Paul says bluntly, "This is the will of God, your sanctification" (1 Thess. 4:3).[10] "To be sanctified," says Ian Thomas, "means that God is able to put us completely to our *correct* use" (*The Mystery of Godliness*, 54).

What good is it to participate in all the right activities, marry the right person, donate the right amount of money, major in the right subject, and go to the right places, if we're not living the right life?[11] Misguided preoccupation with God's will in things like jobs and errands easily becomes an alternative to making mature decisions. It is also easily perverted into the vacuous philosophy that whatever happens must be God's will, and that however we feel, must be His leading. We thereby trivialize God's will into imagined whims.

Not only does God not normally intervene in our circumstances, He does not normally tell us specifically what to do in them. The question is not whether God's will is that we be here or there doing this or that; the question is whether we are willing to be His man or woman *wherever* we may be and *whatever* our circumstances.

1. One conspicuous apparent exception to the suggestion that God has no individual ad hoc will for us is the recurring statement in the New Testament, "I will do such and such if God wills" (Acts 18:21; Rom. 1:10; and others). It usually refers to Paul's travel plans. The idea is spelled out by James in a passage quoted frequently in discussions about God's individual will: "Come now, you who say, 'Today or tomorrow, we shall go to such and such a city, and spend a year there and engage in business and make a profit.' Yet you do not know what your life will be like tomorrow. You are just a vapor that appears for a little while and then vanishes away. Instead, you ought to say, 'If the Lord wills, we shall live and also do this or that.' But as it is, you boast in your arrogance; all such boasting is evil" (James 4:13–16).

James' point is not that God wills you to do this or that, but that you don't know the future and may not be alive tomorrow to do anything. So don't be arrogant in your planning. James gives no hint that God might prefer that you do something *else* tomorrow. He tells us less here about God's will than about living with God's perspective and getting our attitudes right.

James' point is the same one Jesus made in saying of the rich man who wanted to build bigger barns, "You fool! This very night your soul is required of you" (Luke 12:15–20). It is the same principle journalists go by when they write that the president "is expected" to do such and such, rather than saying that he *will* do it. It was a lesson Peter needed to learn when he said to Jesus, "Even though all may fall away because of You, I will never fall away" (Matt. 26:33). Paul had learned the lesson, so he often (though not always) added the qualification "if God wills" when talking about his plans. We shouldn't read too much more into it.

2. Garry Friesen writes that the traditional view of seeking God's individual will promotes immature decisions in the following ways:

> "By permitting believers to justify unwise decisions on grounds that 'God told me to do it.'
>
> "By fostering costly delays because of uncertainty about God's individual will.
>
> "By influencing people to reject personal preferences when faced with apparently equal options.
>
> "By encouraging the practice of 'putting out a fleece'—letting circumstances dictate the decision."
>
> (*Decision Making and the Will of God,* 126)

3. Likewise in the Old Testament, the instances of guidance are pretty much confined to prophets, kings, judges, and others with some special role in

God's work. David's experiences with guidance are discussed in chapter 5, "Believing Jacob's Lie."

4. Garry Friesen, *Decision Making*, 90.

5. For more detail, see Friesen, part 2, 81-147. "A well-known feature of compulsive neurotics," says Erich Fromm, is that "when afraid of the outcome of an important undertaking [they] may, while awaiting an answer, count the windows of houses or trees on the street. If the number is even, a person feels that things will be all right; if it is uneven, it is a sign that he will fail. Frequently this doubt does not refer to a specific instance but to a person's whole life, and the compulsion to look for 'signs' will pervade it accordingly" (*Escape From Freedom*, 92).

6. 2 Corinthians 6:14; Hebrews 10:25.

7. Romans 12:2.

8. 2 Timothy 1:7 KJV; 1 Corinthians 2:16.

9. Hebrews 5:14; James 1:5; 3:17.

10. Paul's overall subject in this passage is sexual morality, a specific application of the broader principle of sanctification.

11. I have a number of friends who are seeking God's leading in finding a house. I hope they all get one; I'd like one myself. But I have a hard time believing that God's will for us involves things like finding a nice house while millions of people throughout the world live in tumble-down shacks. They would love an apartment as grand as the one I consider inadequate. We in an affluent society so easily slip into a pattern of seeking God's leading about whether He wants us to have, in effect, lobster tails or baked salmon, when about the only biblical support we'll find is for daily bread. Do we really have any business invoking God to justify our own preferences?

18.   PRAYER

We can't talk about how God operates in people's lives without talking about prayer, because the way we pray is the surest indication of what we really believe about how He operates. In prayer we ask Him to do the kinds of things we believe He is in the business of doing. If we ask Him to forgive our sins, it is because we believe He does that sort of thing. If we ask Him to give us microwave ovens or get so-and-so a job or move people around to our liking, then we must believe (or at least hope) that those are among the kinds of things He does. Conversely, if we don't believe He normally turns people who annoy us into pumpkins, we are not liable to ask Him to.

As our conceptions of God's character and ways change, our prayer habits are bound to change accordingly.[1] Such changes can be unsettling, but there is danger if we interpret that change to mean we should stop praying altogether. I am sometimes asked, "If you don't believe God works in circumstances, then why pray?" We could ask Calvin or Luther the corresponding question: "If you believe God already determines, causes, and controls everything to the nth degree anyway, then why pray?"

Neither question is valid, though, because both rest on the implicit assumption that asking for God's intervention in circumstances is what prayer is all about—and that if we subtracted that element, there would be little or nothing left. In fact there should be *plenty* left: praise, worship, confession, thanksgiving for what God really has done, asking for inner growth, communing with our Abba Father, and just talking things over.

The question, "Why pray?" also misses the whole point of

this book. Prayer is vital for our inner spiritual growth, which is one of our purposes in life. When we come to recognize that God operates in our inner being rather than in our circumstances, the appropriate response is to pray more avidly and candidly, not to stop praying altogether.

God delights in our prayers,[2] but prayer is primarily for our own benefit, not God's. He knows what we need and want long before we pray;[3] prayer is the process of aligning our will, our attitudes, and our perspective with His. This is the only way we could possibly "pray without ceasing" (1 Thess. 5:17). Praying should make us willing to be the answer to our own prayers: so we would pass from praying, "Send someone," to saying, "I'll volunteer." The result of prayer, therefore, should be a deeper and refreshed sense of agreement with God. In other words, the purpose of prayer is not to talk God into things or to change our circumstances, but to change *us*.

We are, of course, still welcome to pray about our circumstances; the question is *what* we pray about them. Praying about them is a way of facing up to them frankly, re-evaluating them, getting new ideas about how to deal with them, changing our attitude about them, and drawing on the strength God is in us to cope.

We are often counseled to lay our troubles at the Lord's feet. That's sound advice, but *why* should we do that? So He can solve our problems for us? No. He's not Santa Claus. When we lay our troubles at His feet, we can begin to put them in perspective. We can begin to remember that *He*—and not our problems—is our master.

When we confess our sin to God, we're not informing Him of anything. We are simply agreeing with Him about it. Confessing sin forces us to acknowledge to ourselves (as we acknowledge to Him) that we are indeed sinners, that we blew it again, and even that, yes, we rather enjoyed it. It forces us to confront ourselves—without paying a psychologist seventy-five dollars an hour. Honest prayer—*honest* prayer—causes us to face up to things like our resentment, hostility, jealousy, and

CIRCUMSTANCES

pride; recognize them for what they are; make appropriate decisions about what to do about them in light of God's Word; confess them; and begin to repent of them.[4]

An attitude of frank, candid prayer gives our Father an opportunity to guide our imagination and creativity, bring things to our attention, remind us of His Word, and point out problems and areas of sin in our lives. Candid prayer precludes trying to keep secrets from God or snow Him. It is a hard-core honesty with Him and with ourselves, which is healthy psychologically. Perhaps most important, it reinforces and refreshes our relationship with our Father.

AGREEING WITH GOD

God does His work in our inner being to change what we value to square with and agree with what He values. The Lord's Prayer illustrates that principle. It consists of four elements:

> worship ("Our Father who art in heaven, hallowed be Thy name," and "Thine is the kingdom and the power, and the glory, forever")
> accord with His will ("Thy kingdom come, Thy will be done, on earth as it is in heaven")
> one simple request ("Give us this day our daily bread")
> dealing with sin ("Forgive us our debts, as we also have forgiven our debtors. And do not lead us into temptation, but deliver us from evil")

Each element is a matter of agreeing with God about something. When we worship, we are agreeing with God about His glory and celebrating it. When we say, "Thy kingdom come, Thy will be done," we are agreeing that He has a right to be our lord and are agreeing to yield personally to His lordship in our lives. To say, "Give us this day our daily bread" is to ask for nothing more (or less) than what He already knows you need and wants you to have.[5] It is also an agreement to be content with bread (rather than expect filet mignon) on a day-by-day basis (rather than have storehouses of surplus).

As for dealing with sin, the very word *confess* means to "say with," or "agree about." God knows perfectly well what we did—He just wants us to recognize it too. By forgiving our neighbors we are agreeing with God's position that one sinner has no business feeling morally superior to another sinner. To repent means to change your mind about your sin, that is, come to agree with God about it.

We can pray in Jesus' name only when—and insofar as— we agree with Him. The problem is that we always want Him to agree with us: like James and John, "we want You to do for us whatever we ask of You" (Mark 10:35). We are, of course, clever enough to tack on the magic charm formula, "in Thy name we pray," just before "amen," since we know the promises about getting whatever we ask for in His name. But praying in His name is a far deeper issue, just as it is to do anything in anybody's name.

For example, I once interviewed the great mime, Marcel Marceau, for a magazine article. A year later, I went to one of his performances and ran into his manager, Jim Hulse, at intermission. Jim recognized me and invited me backstage to say hello to Marceau after the performance. When I got to the stage door, a dozen other people were trying to get in, but a guard kept everyone out. Everyone else was saying, "I just want a quick autograph," or, "I just want a picture," but I said, "Jim Hulse invited me." The guard immediately let me in.

I entered in Jim's name. I got what I wanted (admission backstage) only because it was what Jim wanted. And had I *not* wanted to go backstage, his invitation would have come to naught. It worked because we were in agreement. No one else outside the door got their request, because theirs were all outside the will of the person in the position to grant their requests. And had I abused my privilege by trying to do something outside Jim's will, I would quickly have found myself back outside the door with everyone else. What mattered, therefore, were Jim's will, his authority with the guard, and the fact that he knew me.

Praying in Jesus' name is sort of like that. He has the standing with the Father for Him to give us what we ask for, but He only promises to give us what He wants us to have. The fact that He wants it for us, though, won't help much unless *we also* want it and therefore appropriate it. To get what we want, then, we must want what He wants for us. And the promise applies only to those whom He knows: He knows His own sheep, but He doesn't know everybody.[6]

To pray in His name effectively, we must have a good sense of how God operates, that is, what kinds of things He normally does and does not do. When we understand how He normally operates, we will begin to avoid meaningless prayers like, "Be with the sick." Is He not "with them" already, whatever that means? Which sick? What benefit do we expect them to derive? Physical healing? Comfort? Less pain? Then pray for that. At least you'll be able to find out whether or not your prayer had any effect. Jesus taught us to pray without long-winded mush.

USING HIS NAME IN VAIN

Suppose I am hurrying to work or class or an appointment. Five miles away from my destination, I realize that I'm just not going to make it on time. If I pray, asking the Lord to get me there on time, what am I really asking Him to do? Make other drivers get off the road to thin out traffic? Freeze the lights so they stay green for me? Expunge from history the fact that I left home late? I would probably be asking Him to do all those unlikely things—while supposing that I was only asking Him to help out His child somehow. With the best of intentions, I would be asking Him to perform all manner of miracles on my behalf—and hang the consequences for everybody else He might be sweeping aside to make way for me.

God has His ways of operating, and we cannot ask *in Jesus' name* that He change them to suit our whims or even for what we consider noble purposes. He is perfectly within His prerogatives to make an exception in a given case to accomplish some purpose of His own, but we have no business asking Him to change His ways to accomplish some purpose of ours.

Yet we routinely—and with the best of intentions—ask Him to do the most extraordinary things: cause someone to make a decision we want (to suspend and overrule that person's capacity to make his or her own decisions), bring certain kinds of people into someone's life (manipulate people), free our communities from crime or pornography or whatever (make things happen independent of human cooperation), make some inanimate object hold out until we're through depending on it (suspend His own laws of physics), or bless our plans (agree with us regardless of whether we agree with Him, which often would require waiving His standards of holiness).

I suspect Jesus often says to us the same thing He said to James and John when they asked Him to do for them whatever they wanted: "You do not know what you are asking for" (Mark 10:38).

Though we are free to pray for anything, we cannot pray for some kinds of things in Jesus' name. Nor should we use His name in vain when trying to talk God into some business transaction, whether of the foxhole variety ("If You'll just do this one thing, I swear I'll go to church more") or the slick gospel gimmick variety ("I'll give the TV preacher $1,000 and You make my kids magically shape up"). As William Barclay says, "Whenever we try to turn prayer into something to enable us to realize our own ambitions and to satisfy our own desires, prayer must be ineffective, for it is not real prayer at all" (*The Gospel of John,* vol. 2, 210).

One of our purposes in life is to become conformed to the image of Christ. To that end, God does His work in our inner being, changing our wants and priorities to correspond to His, that is, to cultivate agreement with Him. We could say, therefore, that agreeing with God is what Christianity ultimately is all about. When we genuinely agree with God about something, we act, in effect, in Jesus' name. Prayer, as a part of our relationship with God, works on the same principle: it too is a matter of agreement—us agreeing with Him. We abuse that principle when we try to talk Him into agreeing with us. That is trying to use Him as a means to our own ends, just as the Pharisees did.

We can pray effectively and intelligently only to the extent that we pray according to how God really operates. This is one reason why studying the Bible is indispensable to Christian growth. To the extent that our requests are based on misconceptions—no matter how sincere—they will be futile.[7]

Our circumstances are certainly among the things we should pray about, but instead of asking Him to make them right for us, we should be asking Him to make us right for them. Before we ask God to do anything, we should first ask ourselves what we're really trying to get Him to do. If we're asking Him to work in a way He normally does not, we are asking in our own name, not Christ's. We waste our time asking Him to agree with us.

On a deeper level, as long as we think of prayer as a session of asking God for things, especially for intervention, we're liable to cheat ourselves out of the greater value of prayer. If, however, we think of prayer as the process of aligning our will, attitudes, and perspective with God's, we may find ourselves doing less asking and more growing.

NOTES

1. Unless, of course, those habits are so firmly entrenched that we don't notice inconsistencies between them and our changing conceptions.

2. Proverbs 15:8.

3. Matthew 6:8, 32.

4. I say "begin to repent" because repentance means to change our minds about our sins. That's a tall order and not something to be approached glibly or superficially.

5. Matthew 6:31–32; 7:9–11.

6. John 10:26–27; Matthew 7:23. See also John 15:7 and chapter 9, "God in You," note 11.

7. Harold Kushner writes about examples from the Talmud of improper prayers. For example, "If a woman is pregnant, neither she nor her husband should pray, 'May God grant that this child be a boy' (nor, for that matter, may they pray that it be a girl). The sex of the child is determined at conception, and God cannot be invoked to change it. Again, if a man sees a fire engine racing toward his neighborhood, he should not pray, 'Please God, don't let the fire be in my house.' Not only is it mean-spirited to pray that someone else's house burn instead of yours, but it is futile. A certain house is already on fire; the most sincere or articulate of prayers will not affect the question of which house it is" (*When Bad Things Happen to Good People*, 115–16).

19.   SO WHAT?

We've covered a lot of territory. Let's tie it all together and see what it adds up to.

The three questions we've addressed are: How do we make sense of our circumstances? How do people operate? and What is—and what is not—God's role in our lives? In the smallest of nutshells, the key to answering all three questions is to recognize the centrality of the free human decision. Our vocation as human beings is to make decisions, our circumstances are the direct result of countless decisions and actions people make, and the objective of God's work in our lives is to develop in us agreement with His values so that the decisions we freely make are godly ones.

The starting point for making sense of circumstances is the principle that things don't happen, but that people do things. Our circumstances consist, with a few kinds of exceptions, of the consequences of decisions people make and things people do. Those consequences intersect, overlap, tangle up, and accumulate randomly. Our circumstances are therefore a web of complex coincidences. There is no such thing as luck, fate, or any other non-intelligent cosmic force coordinating or guiding our circumstances. Each decision, event, and situation is a point on a continuum. No matter how many people are involved, how many decisions and actions created it, how far back they go, or how good or bad those decisions and actions were, our circumstances are people's doing.

We don't always make decisions, but when we do, our decisions can usually be accounted for by either of two basic criteria: we either do precisely what we want to do, or we do what is most important to us at the moment we make the decision. Something we decide not to do may not be *un*important to us; there may just be something else we consider *more* important. Any number of things may influence our system of wants and priorities, but these wants and priorities are the direct basis of our behavior.

What we value may not be simple or obvious. While we do many things that we don't value for themselves, we do them because they are means to some end that we *do* value. Often the choice we face is not between a simple this or that, but between this and the *risk* of that. In such cases, the greater the risk we perceive, the lower that option will be in our priorities. Our wants and priorities change with time, so any given decision is like a snapshot of our wants and priorities at the moment we make the decision.

One of the key themes of the Bible, therefore, is: Get your priorities straight. It applies both on the grand scale (making the Lord first priority) and on a decision-by-decision scale. The heart of our spiritual problem is not what we do, but what we want.

Though we say we do what we do because we have to, the fact is that no one can force you to do anything you do not consent to do. The only leverage anyone can exert on you is to exploit your own wants and priorities. If, however, you insist on sticking to a priority higher than the one they appeal to, you are free to do so. Declining to cooperate may be godly and heroic or it may be stupid and suicidal, but we always have choices and are always free to make our own choices. We can do anything, regardless of its merits, that requires only a decision on our own part to do. But, just as no one can force you to cooperate with them, neither can you force them to cooperate with you to accomplish your goals. God cannot "give you success" in any endeavor that requires other people's cooperation without depriving them of their capacity to decide.

Clear priorities come from a clear sense of purpose. Our biblical purposes in life can be summarized as becoming conformed to the image of Christ and bearing His fruit of love.

These are the ends toward which God does His work in us. We are useless to God if we are not loving, but loving always accomplishes His will and satisfies His demands. The commandments to love the Lord and to love our neighbor are the two greatest because they call on us to get our priorities straight and to fulfill our purpose in life.

The ways God operates in our lives mesh perfectly with the ways He designed us to operate. He does not normally determine, cause, and control our circumstances, because He could do so only by controlling *us* to the *n*th degree. He does not, for instance, give us jobs or customers, rig elections, or cause certain people to be in certain places at certain times. Circumstances are people's doing, not God's. He *can* intervene in them, He *has*, and on occasion He may choose to—but He normally does not. His kingdom is not of this world.

If, as many Christians believe, God *did* normally determine, cause, and control our circumstances, His fruits would reveal Him to be morally ambivalent at best and malevolent at worst—not our loving Father, but our most fearsome enemy. The idea that He might determine the outcome of something while leaving us free to produce that outcome is nonsense: He can't cause an ultimate effect without causing the *cause* of that effect. If He did determine all outcomes, He would also be causing such obvious evils as rapes, child abuse, and wars, but He would also be defeating His own purposes by causing events calculated to push people away from Himself and destroying their faith. He would be causing all the very misery He wants Christians to alleviate. There would be good reason to fear Him, but no reason to love or worship Him.

God is indeed sovereign, but His sovereignty does not require that He exercise total control of everything everybody does. It is diminished not a whit by granting autonomy to creatures, who make their own decisions, reap the consequences of what they sow, and thereby create their own circumstances. For God to "send" circumstances would be a clumsy, ineffective way to accomplish His purposes since most do *not* learn spiritual lessons from their experiences.

Not only does He not cause or bail us out of our circumstances, neither does He tell us what to do in them. We have such a hard time divining His individual will for us—shall I do this or that? go here or there?—because no such ad hoc will exists. God's will is about sweeping, fundamental things like salvation and sanctification, not about details like which apartment to rent. His will for us, in a word, is that we fulfill His purpose for us: that we become like Jesus and bear His fruit of love. He equips us inwardly to make our own intelligent, mature, godly decisions—a capacity we waste when we wait for Him to whisper in our ear.

God does His work not in our circumstances, but in our innermost being. The Holy Spirit's job is to change the inner essence of what we are, make us new creatures, and replace our values with His. He does what He does with us *as believers*, that is, He makes us better Christians, not better electricians or golfers. He helps us understand His Word, inspires words and ideas (specifically, those related to the gospel), and produces in us whatever Christian virtues we may exhibit. Gradually but persistently, He chisels us into the image of Christ—but He works only by our permission at each turn. We can stop Him whenever we please. We might prefer that He do His work on temporal, external things like our circumstances, but He concentrates instead on the only thing that's going to last into eternity, our inner being.

As we allow Him to do His work in us, He changes our wants and priorities, so that ours begin to give way to His. We come to agree with Him. His will becomes our own will. And we are invariably true to what we ourselves genuinely value.

We can pray effectively only insofar as we pray according to how God really operates. We can pray in Jesus' name only insofar as we agree with Him. Prayer is not a matter of asking Him to intervene in our circumstances, but is above all the process of aligning our priorities, attitudes, and perspective with His. The result of prayer, therefore, is not convincing God to agree with us, but our coming to agree with Him, which is what Christianity is all about.

WHERE DOES IT LEAVE US?

The ultimate philosophical question is, "So what?" Where does the perspective we've discussed leave us?

If we apply the perspective consistently, we can become more honest and straightforward toward ourselves, toward others, toward God, and toward our circumstances. By getting rid of the assumption that God is controlling our circumstances, we can save ourselves a lot of needless misery and confusion. By recognizing our own wants and priorities, we come to know ourselves better. We face up to our responsibility to ourselves, to one another, and to God for the decisions we make and the things we do. We can either reconcile ourselves to our choices or make new choices that we can better live with. We can forthrightly recognize the things that "happen" to us for what they really are, rather than splash about in the bitterness and resentment bred of superstition.

This perspective undercuts our excuses for settling for mediocrity, insincerity, and failure. It can provide a catalyst to snap us out of a mindset that keeps us spiritual babes, unwilling to make mature decisions. We breathe brisk air when we realize that we can break free of imaginary constraints and unwarranted assumptions. It can often help immensely just to realize that you have a decision to make, that that's what the situation calls for. We can make wiser decisions when we become aware of the wants and priorities behind them and of the ends we are really pursuing when we choose a given means.

My fervent hope is that this perspective will make us think twice before saying such nonsense as, "God was so gracious in arranging for me to get this job," or, "I guess this tragedy was just God's will."

The perspective answers questions as diverse as what our purposes in life are, why we are saved by grace instead of by works of law, why many prayers have no effect, why we procrastinate, why God holds us eternally responsible for what we do with our time on earth, why He allows evil in the world, and why bad things "happen" to us. It can provide a healthy perspective on guilt and on God's will and can help us pray more effectively and meaningfully. It may or may not make us *feel* better about our circumstances, but it should help us make sense of them.

In the end it should also help us realize the need to get our priorities straight. In both the life-scale policies and the scratchy minute-to-minute choices, we live the human life based upon what we want and what is important to us. To live the *Christian* life, we must voluntarily allow God to develop in us an ever deeper agreement with His wants and priorities, so that His become our own. To the extent that we agree with God, we will make godly decisions. To the extent that we make godly decisions, we will live godly lives.

Appendix   *Biblical Statements of Purpose in Life*

Refer to chapter 12 for the use of this index.

CHRIST'S PURPOSES FOR COMING TO EARTH

TO DEAL WITH SIN

Save sinners: "Jesus came into the world to save sinners" (1 Tim. 1:15).

Save the world: "I did not come to judge the world, but to save the world" (John 12:47; see also John 3:17).

Put away sin: Jesus "has been manifested to put away sin by the sacrifice of Himself" (Heb. 9:26).

Take away sins: "He appeared in order to take away sins" (1 John 3:5).

Die for us: He came "that by the grace of God He might taste death for every one" (Heb. 2:9; see also John 12:27).

Call sinners to repentance: "I have not come to call righteous men but sinners to repentance" (Luke 5:32).

Offer eternal life: "God . . . gave His only begotten Son, that whoever believes in Him should not perish, but have eternal life" (John 3:16).

Be propitiation: God "sent His Son to be the propitiation for our sins" (1 John 4:10).

Destroy works of devil: "The Son of God appeared for this purpose, that He might destroy the works of the devil" (1 John 3:8).

Redeem and adopt: God sent Jesus "in order that He might redeem those who were under the Law, that we might receive the adoption as sons" (Gal. 4:5).

TO GIVE US LIFE

Offer abundant life: "I came that they might have life, and might have it abundantly" (John 10:10).

We live through Him: "God has sent His only begotten Son into the world so that we might live through Him" (1 John 4:9).

We receive the Spirit: "Christ redeemed us from the curse of the Law ... in order that in Christ Jesus the blessing of Abraham might come to the Gentiles, so that we might receive the promise of the Spirit through faith" (Gal. 3:13–14).

TO ENLIGHTEN

Witness of truth: "For this I have been born, and for this I have come into the world, to bear witness to the truth" (John 18:37).

To preach: "Let us go somewhere else to the towns nearby, in order that I may preach there also; for that is what I came out for" (Mark 1:38).

Preach release, recovery, liberation: God anointed Jesus "to preach the gospel to the poor. He has sent Me to proclaim release to the captives, and recovery of sight to the blind, to set free those who are downtrodden, to proclaim the favorable year of the Lord" (Luke 4:18–19; Isa. 61:1–2).

Judge and enlighten: "For judgment I came into this world, that those who do not see may see; and that those who see may become blind" (John 9:39).

Be light: "I have come as light into the world, that everyone who believes in Me may not remain in darkness" (John 12:46).

Let us know God: "The Son of God has come, and has given us understanding, in order that we might know Him who is true, and we are in Him who is true, in His Son Jesus Christ" (1 John 5:20; see also 4:7).

MISCELLANEOUS

To serve: "The Son of Man did not come to be served, but to serve, and to give His life a ransom for many" (Matt. 20:28).

Fulfill the law: "Do not think that I came to abolish the Law or the Prophets; I did not come to abolish, but to fulfill" (Matt. 5:17).

Cast fire, divide: "I have come to cast fire upon the earth. . . . Do you suppose that I came to grant peace on earth? I tell you, no, but rather division [that is, households divided]" (Luke 12:49, 51).

JESUS' PURPOSES IN DYING

DELIVER US

Render devil powerless: He came "that through death He might render powerless . . . the devil" (Heb. 2:14).

Deliver from evil age: Jesus "gave Himself for our sins, that He might deliver us out of this present evil age" (Gal. 1:4).

Deliver slaves of fear: He died that He "might deliver those who through fear of death were subject to slavery all their lives" (Heb. 2:15).

ESTABLISH HIS LORDSHIP

Bring us to God: Christ died "in order that He might bring us to God" (1 Peter 3:18).

We live for Him: "He died for all, that they who live should no longer live for themselves, but for Him" (2 Cor. 5:15).

Be Lord: "For to this end Christ died and lived again, that He might be Lord both of the dead and of the living" (Rom. 14:9).

We live with Him: He "died for us, that whether we are awake or asleep, we may live together with Him" (1 Thess. 5:10).

Have first place: "He is . . . the first-born from the dead; so that He Himself might come to have first place in everything" (Col. 1:18).

MAKE US HOLY, RIGHTEOUS

We live to righteousness: He bore our sins "that we might die to sin and live to righteousness" (1 Peter 2:24).

We become righteous: "He made Him who knew no sin to be sin on our behalf, that we might become the righteousness of God in Him" (2 Cor. 5:21).

Redeem, purify us: Jesus "gave Himself for us, that He might redeem us from every lawless deed and purify for Himself a people for His own possession, zealous for good deeds" (Titus 2:14).

Sanctify, cleanse, purify us: He gave Himself up for the church "that He might sanctify her, having cleansed her by the washing of water with the word, that He might present to Himself the church in all her glory, having no spot or wrinkle or any such thing; but that she should be holy and blameless" (Eph. 5:25–27).

Make us holy, blameless: "He has now reconciled you in His fleshly body through death, in order to present you before Him holy and blameless and beyond reproach" (Col. 1:22).

Sanctify us: "Jesus also, that He might sanctify the people through His own blood, suffered outside the gate" (Heb. 13:12).

PAUL'S PURPOSES

Build believers to maturity: God gave apostles, prophets, evangelists, pastors, and teachers "for the equipping of the saints for the work of service, to the building up of the body of Christ; until we all attain to the unity of the faith, and of the knowledge of the Son of God, to a mature man, to the measure of the stature which belongs to the fulness of Christ. As a result, we are . . . to grow up in all aspects into Him, who is the head, even Christ" (Eph. 4:11–15; see also 2 Cor. 12:19).

Preach, present believers complete: "I was made a minister . . . that I might fully carry out the preaching of the word of God,

that is, [God's long-hidden mystery, now revealed] ...
which is Christ in you, the hope of glory. [And we teach]
that we may present every man complete in Christ. And
for this purpose also I labor" (Col. 1:25–29).

That we be encouraged and know Christ: I struggle "that their
hearts may be encouraged, having been knit together in
love, and attaining to all the wealth that comes from the
full assurance of understanding, resulting in a true
knowledge of God's mystery, that is, Christ Himself"
(Col. 2:2).

Christ formed in us: "My children, with whom I am again in
labor until Christ is formed in you" (Gal 4:19).

That we walk worthily: We exhort, encourage, and implore "so
that you may walk in a manner worthy of the God who
calls you" (1 Thess. 2:11–12).

Love, conscience, faith: "The goal of our instruction is love from a
pure heart and a good conscience and a sincere faith"
(1 Tim. 1:5).

OUR PURPOSES IN LIFE

Created for God's pleasure: "O Lord, ... thou hast created all
things, and for thy pleasure they are and were created"
(Rev. 4:11 KJV).

Be pleasing to God: "We groan, longing to be clothed with our
dwelling from heaven ... in order that what is mortal
may be swallowed up by life. Now He who prepared us
for this very purpose is God. ... Therefore also we have
as our ambition, whether at home [with the Lord] or
absent, to be pleasing to Him" (2 Cor. 5:2–9).

Show us His grace: God made us alive with Christ, raised us with
Him, "and seated us with Him in the heavenly places, in
Christ Jesus, in order that in the ages to come He might
show the surpassing riches of His grace in kindness
toward us in Christ Jesus" (Eph. 2:4–7).

Gain Christ's glory: "And it was for this He called you through
our gospel, that you may gain the glory of our Lord Jesus
Christ" (2 Thess. 2:14).

Be to the praise of His glory: God predestined us "according to His purpose . . . to the end that we who were the first to hope in Christ should be to the praise of His glory" (Eph. 1:11–12; see also John 15:8 and Matt. 5:16).

For God's glory: "I have created him for my glory" (Isa. 43:7 KJV).

Bear fruit: We died to law, have been joined to Christ "that we might bear fruit for God" (Rom. 7:4).

Bear more fruit: "Every branch that bears fruit, He prunes it, that it may bear more fruit" (John 15:2).

Fruit should remain: "I chose you, and appointed you, that you should go and bear fruit, and that your fruit should remain" (John 15:16).

Good works: "We are His workmanship, created in Christ Jesus for good works, which God prepared beforehand, that we should walk in them" (Eph. 2:10).

Be holy and blameless sons: "He chose us in Him before the foundation of the world, that we should be holy and blameless before Him. In love He predestined us to adoption as sons through Jesus Christ to Himself" (Eph. 1:4–5).

Be heirs: "He saved us . . . that being justified by His grace we might be made heirs" (Titus 3:5, 7).

Be saved, gain glory of Jesus: "God has chosen you from the beginning for salvation through sanctification by the Spirit and faith in the truth. And it was for this He called you through our gospel, that you may gain the glory of our Lord Jesus Christ" (2 Thess. 2:13–14).

Suffer for doing right: "But if when you do what is right and suffer for it you patiently endure it, this finds favor with God. For you have been called for this purpose, since Christ also suffered for you, leaving you an example for you to follow in His steps" (1 Peter 2:20–21).

Obtain salvation: "God has not destined us for wrath, but for obtaining salvation through our Lord Jesus Christ" (1 Thess. 5:9).

Sanctification: "For God has not called us for the purpose of impurity, but in sanctification" (1 Thess. 4:7).

New life: "We have been buried with Him through baptism into death, in order that as Christ was raised from the dead through the glory of the Father, so we too might walk in newness of life" (Rom. 6:4).

Dominion over earth: "Thou madest him [man] to have dominion over the works of thy hands; thou hast put all things under his feet: all sheep and oxen, yea, and the beasts of the field" (Psalm 8:6–7 KJV).

BIBLIOGRAPHY

Barclay, William. *The Gospel of John*, vol. 2. *The Daily Study Bible*. Philadelphia: Westminster Press, 1955.

————. *The Letters to the Galatians and Ephesians*, 2nd ed. *The Daily Study Bible*. Philadelphia: Westminster Press, 1958.

Barth, Markus. *Ephesians: Introduction, Translation, and Commentary on Chapters 1–3*. Garden City: Doubleday and Co., 1974.

Bromiley, Geoffrey W. *Historical Theology: An Introduction*. Grand Rapids: Wm. B. Eerdmans Publishing Co., 1978.

Cullmann, Oscar. *The State in the New Testament*. New York: Charles Scribner's Sons, 1956.

Douglas, J. D., ed. *The New Bible Dictionary*. Grand Rapids: Wm. B. Eerdmans Publishing Co., 1962.

Duncan, Ronald, ed. *Gandhi: Selected Writings*. Harper Colophon Books. New York: Harper and Row, Publishers, 1972.

Flesch, Rudolph. *The Art of Plain Talk*. New York: Collier Books, a division of Macmillan Publishing Company, Inc., 1951.

Friesen, Garry, with Maxson, J. Robin. *Decision Making and the Will of God: A Biblical Alternative to the Traditional View*. Portland: Multnomah Press, 1980.

Fromm, Erich. *The Art of Loving*. Perennial Library. New York: Harper and Row, Publishers, 1956.

————. *Escape From Freedom*. New York: Holt, Rinehart and Winston, 1941.

Fuchs, Victor R. *How We Live*. Cambridge, Mass.: Harvard University Press, 1983.

Glover, Jonathan. *Responsibility*. International Library of Philosophy and Scientific Method, Ted Honderich, ed. London: Routledge and Kegan Paul, New York Humanities Press, 1970.

Guelich, Robert A. *The Sermon on the Mount: A Foundation for Understanding*. Waco, Tex.: Word Books, 1982.

Hastings, James, ed. *The Encyclopaedia of Religion and Ethics*. New York: Charles Scribner's Sons, 1955.

Howard, J. Grant Jr. *Knowing God's Will and Doing It!* Grand Rapids: Zondervan Publishing House, 1976.

Hunter, Archibald M. *A Pattern for Life: An Exposition of the Sermon on the Mount, Its Making, Its Exegesis and Its Meaning*, rev. ed. Philadelphia: Westminster Press, 1953.

Jeremias, Joachim. *The Sermon on the Mount*. Translated by Norman Perrin. Facet Books, Biblical Series 2, John Reumann, gen. ed. Philadelphia: Fortress Press, 1963.

Karnow, Stanley. *Vietnam: A History*. New York: The Viking Press, 1983. Published in conjunction with a 1983 PBS program, "Vietnam, A Television History."

Kushner, Harold S. *When Bad Things Happen to Good People*. New York: Avon Books, 1983.

Lewis, C. S. *Mere Christianity*. Macmillan Paperback ed. New York: Macmillan Company, 1960.

_____. *The Problem of Pain*. Macmillan Paperback ed. New York: Macmillan Publishing Co., 1962.

Lindley, D. V. *Making Decisions*. London: John Wiley and Sons, 1971.

Milgram, Stanley. *Obedience to Authority: An Experimental View*. New York: Harper and Row, 1974.

Ryle, J. C. *Ryle's Expository Thoughts on the Gospels*, vol. 3, John 1:1–John 10:30. Grand Rapids: Baker Book House, 1977.

Schmidt, Jerry A. *Do You Hear What You're Thinking?* Wheaton, Ill.: Victor Books, 1983.

Searle, John. *Intentionality*. Cambridge: Cambridge University Press, 1983.

Stansky, Peter, ed. *On Nineteen Eighty-Four*. The Portable Stanford. Stanford, Cal.: Stanford Alumni Association, 1983.

Thomas, Major W. Ian. *The Mystery of Godliness*. Grand Rapids: Zondervan Publishing House, 1964.

_____. *The Saving Life of Christ*. Grand Rapids: Zondervan Publishing House, 1961.

Vine, W. E. *Vine's Expository Dictionary of New Testament Words*. McLean, Virg.: MacDonald Publishing Co., n.d.

Weiss, G. Christian. *The Perfect Will of God*. Chicago: Moody Press, 1950.

Winter, Ernst F., trans. and ed. *Erasmus-Luther: Discourse on Free Will*. Milestones of Thought in the History of Ideas. Strothmann, F.W., and Locke, Frederick W., gen. eds. New York: Frederick Unger Publishing Co., 1961.

INDEX